W9-BVJ-300

How To

TEACH READING

For Teachers
Parents
Tutors

by Edward Fry, Ph.D.
Professor Emeritus
Rutgers University

Laguna Beach
Educational Books
245 Grandview
Laguna Beach, CA 92651

HOW TO TEACH READING
For Teachers, Parents, Tutors

Laguna Beach Educational Books
245 Grandview
Laguna Beach, CA 92651
Ph: (714) 494-4225 Fax: (714) 494-2403

Published by Laguna Beach Educational Books
Copyright ©1995 by Edward Fry
Printed in the United States of America
by Victor Graphics, Baltimore MD
Edited by Reta Holmback
Typography by Käthe Sheldon

ISBN   0-87673-023-3
Library of Congress Catalogue Card No. 92-072076

TABLE OF CONTENTS

PREFACE

The first draft of this manual was developed at the Graduate School of Education at Rutgers University for a group of Peace Corps volunteers in training on campus. Their schedules were so crowded that little time was allotted for lectures on "How to Teach Reading" so I thought it best to give them something to carry into the field when needed.

I later discovered that there were many people who wanted to know how to teach reading and who didn't want to take a full university course, or even read a thick teacher's textbook. So I rewrote the first draft into this little manual.

This book has been used by thousands of parents, adult literacy tutors, volunteers for disadvantaged programs, teachers' aides, and even classroom teachers who want a rapid overview of some proven methods of teaching reading. It has also been used by college students in laboratory and clinic type teacher training courses.

This current revision is necessary because of some changes in the reading field. These changes include more emphasis on the use of better literature for story content, and more emphasis on writing. This new manual also has longer lists of phonic words, high frequency words, and lists of reading materials. But basically, the 6 Steps given in this manual have stood the test of time, and I am pleased to say they have helped many thousands of students read better.

Edward Fry, Ph.D.
Professor Emeritus
Rutgers University

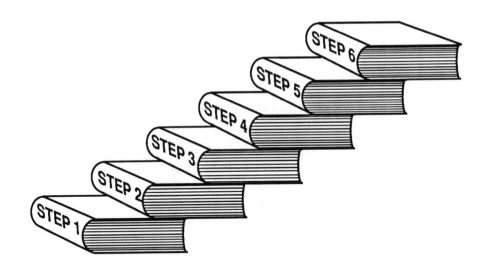

HOW TO TEACH READING

How do you teach a child or an adult to read?

This is an easy question and a difficult question. I can tell you in a sentence. I can tell you in a paragraph. I can tell you in a chapter. I can tell you in a whole book. And there would still be much more to be said.

But just to make my opening statement true, here is a one sentence description of how you teach a student to read.

"You teach a student to read by helping him to learn the relationship between the printed words and their meanings."

You might say that that is not much of an explanation, and you are correct. But this explanation states a very fundamental concept underlying most reading instruction.

Now let's try a one-paragraph answer to the opening question.

"The teaching of reading usually begins by presenting the student with a story that has simple vocabulary arranged in short, easy sentences in a book or on a chart. The student

is given help and is encouraged to practice reading these aloud and silently. More words are added to the reading material, and the sentences and stories get longer. Phonics skills are taught. This means teaching the relationship between letters and sounds. Comprehension skills are taught usually by having the student read silently and answer various types of questions. Writing is introduced; the student starts to write and read his own stories. The printed stories, student-written stories, phonics lessons, and comprehension drills gradually increase in difficulty as the student gains in ability. Usually quite a bit of reading practice and frequent review lessons are necessary."

I hope that you found the one-paragraph explanation of teaching reading more satisfactory. But I will admit that it still does not give you too much insight into the reading process or specific methods of teaching reading. So we will now give you the one-chapter explanation which will be followed by some additional information.

This booklet is written from the standpoint of a teacher, tutor or parent working with an individual student. Certainly, many of the methods discussed here apply to small groups or even classrooms, but to understand the reading process, we must consider what happens to "a student", not some vague thing called "a group".

The methods in this book are suitable for beginning readers and remedial readers of any age from 5 or 6 year olds up through adults. The reading skills needed are the same for any beginning reader - simple reading material, learning common words, phonics, and comprehension. The main difference between young children, teenagers, and adults is in the content of the stories. For example, young children might like to read fairy tales, while older readers prefer football games.

Step 1. Determine the Student's Reading Ability

The first thing to determine is the present reading level of the student. Do not go by his size[1], his age, how many years he has been in school, or other factors which have only a general correlation with reading skills. Find out for yourself as closely as possible what level of material the student can successfully read. This can be quickly and easily done by using the Oral Reading Test and other informal methods which will be discussed in the Step 1 section.

SAMPLE ORAL READING TEST

Here is an example from the Oral Reading Test.

Easy 1st Grade Difficulty
Look at the dog.
It is big.
It can run.
Run dog, run away.

5th Grade Difficulty
High in the hills they came to a wide ledge where trees grew among the rocks. Grass grew in patches and the ground was covered with bits of wood from trees blown over a long time ago and dried by the sun. Down in the valley it was already beginning to get dark.

For the full Oral Reading Test plus instructions on administering it, see the Step 1 section.

---

[1]Footnote. For convenience, masculine pronouns refer to the student and feminine pronouns refer to the teacher throughout the manual.

Step 2. Select the Right Material for the Student to Read

After you have determined your student's reading ability level, select or create reading material of the appropriate level. You can determine the grade level for any story you think he should read by simply using the Readability Graph (page 23). In other words, what this first step is telling you to do is to match the reading ability of the student with the difficulty level of the material. You really need to do a careful and accurate job of matching because the further you miss the match, the more difficult your teaching job will be, and the closer the match, the easier it will be.

Another useful way of determining whether the reading material is at the proper level for the student is simply to ask him to read a bit of it aloud. If he makes more than one mistake in every twenty words, the material is too hard for him. If he makes less than one mistake in every twenty words, he should be able to read it silently with reasonable ease. If he makes about one mistake in every twenty words, then this material is at his instructional level. Material at the instructional level can be used in oral reading lessons or for silent reading where someone is close at hand to help him with difficult words. Do not use material that is too difficult. It blocks learning, makes the student frustrated, and makes your job harder.

JUDGING BOOK DIFFICULTY BY STUDENTS' ORAL READING ERRORS

Less than 1 mistake in 20 words   = Independent Reading Level
Good for silent reading practice and recreational reading.

About 1 mistake in 20 words   = Instructional Level
Good for reading with teacher's or friend's help.

More than 1 mistake in 20 words   = Frustration Level
Don't use. Get an easier book.

It is, of course, very desirable to have interesting reading material. Students like to read about fancy automobiles, sports, adventure, interesting careers, romance (if older), mysteries and stories about their heritage. They also like to read notes and stories you write for them, their own stories, and fellow students' stories.

Step 3. Have the Student Read Aloud and Silently with Comprehension

After you have found the student's reading ability level and matched it with the correct reading material, what do you do? You have him read it aloud, helping him as often as necessary. You also must have him practice reading silently, helping him if he needs it. This can be done alone or in groups.

Keep these practice lessons short so the student does not become bored or frustrated. Schedule them regularly and frequently. For student interest, reading material is often presented on charts, games, pamphlets, or cards; it doesn't really matter how it is presented as long as it is at the right level and your student is comprehending it.

There is no point in having your student read aloud or silently if he doesn't understand what he is reading. The purpose of reading is to receive the author's ideas.

With beginning readers, teaching comprehension is usually not too difficult. Their speaking and listening vocabularies are so far above their reading vocabulary that comprehension takes place almost automatically when you show them the relationship between written and spoken language.

However, within just a few years of reading development, comprehension becomes a major concern and usually must specifically be taught. Written or oral questions following silent or oral reading is the usual method.

Children simply can't learn to read with comprehension unless they practice. It takes practice to learn to read orally and silently and to comprehend. Do not, however, make this an excuse for giving a lot of boring drills.

You can use variety to keep the reading lesson moving on. Go from oral reading to silent reading comprehension drills to the methods suggested in Steps 4 and 5 for teaching the Instant Words (a basic sight word list) and phonics. I often tell teachers to have three or four different kinds of reading activity per hour. Schedule regular lesson periods and stick to them, come hell or high water, riots or baseball games.

Of course, one of the best methods of practice is simply to get a book that the student is interested in and let him read. Usually, to get a student to read silently for a long period of time, you must give him a book that is a little on the easy side. For silent pleasure reading, help the student select a book that is easier than you would use for instruction. Your encouragement, visits to the library, assignment of oral or written book reports, and so on, will encourage your student to read on his own.

Step 4. Teach Vocabulary

For children and all learners, things to be taught are usually presented in a graded order of difficulty, with easiest things first.

Much work has been done in the reading field to determine the proper vocabulary and its order of presentation for the teaching of reading. This is the strong point of most major series of reading texts. They begin with a very few words in the first little book (seventeen in some pre-primers) and gradually increase the vocabulary load. This vocabulary load increase can be seen on the last few pages of most children's reading texts. So, teachers using a traditional basic reading series have a built-in graduated vocabulary. Many modern teachers now use trade books and predictable books for beginners. See Step 4 section.

However, in remedial reading, individualized reading, and literature-based reading programs, it is a good idea to supplement and cross-check on normal vocabulary development and have some systematic list of new words to be taught. Such a list, the Instant Words, will be discussed in a later section.

INSTANT WORDS

Here are the 10 most used words in the English language. If you can't read these, you can't read much. One of them appears in almost every sentence.

the	in
of	is
and	you
a	that
to	it

For more Instant Words and how to teach them, see the Step 4 Section.

The Instant Words are the most common words in the English language. They are arranged in order of frequency of occurrence in reading material and in children's writing. A student should learn to recognize them instantly in order to have ease in reading because they occur so very often. The first one hundred words make up almost one half of all reading material.

You can use the Instant Word Test on page 64. It will tell you which group of Instant Words to start teaching. These may be taught by having your student listen to them, review them, take spelling lessons on them, play card games with them, and so on. Many methods of teaching Instant Words will be given in a later section.

Step 5. Develop Phonics Skills

Basically we have a phonetic language. This means that letters and some letter groups have regular speech sounds. There are plenty of exceptions, but every good reader should know at least the basic phonics principles. Phonics skills are a tremendous help to older students in learning how to read. They are also helpful in spelling lessons and in using the dictionary.

There are phonics charts with carefully chosen example words in Chapter 5 which will help you in teaching all the major phonetic rules. And the Phonics Survey (test) will help you quickly find which main phonics skills the student knows or doesn't know.

Exactly when to begin the teaching of phonics is an emotionally loaded question. Research results are inconclusive. In the vacuum, most people substitute hot arguments. Personally, I think it should begin in kindergarten under the guise of reading readiness activities (playing with letters, coloring them, and mentioning their sounds) and under the guise of speech correction (poems that emphasize different speech sounds). In any event, I would have regular phonics lessons at the first grade level and teach a pretty complete line by the third grade level with some repetition, remedial lessons, and fine points taught even later.

Phonics is taught as part of a spelling program in many parts of the country. It doesn't make any difference what you call it as long as the student learns the relationship between the letters and the sounds. In phonics, as in everything else, you start where the student is and then you test, teach, test again, and teach some more.

> ## PHONICS EXAMPLES
>
> The basic idea in phonics instruction is to help the immature reader learn the connection between letters or letter groups and their speech sounds.
>
> | Similar Beginning Letter | Similar Vowel Sound | Phonograms |
> |:---:|:---:|:---:|
> | /k/ | /ī/ | /-it/ |
> | | | |
> | kind | five | bit |
> | keep | ride | sit |
> | kill | time | hit |
> | key | like | fit |
>
> For teaching suggestions and more phonics charts see the Step 5 Section.

Step 6. Writing

In former years many schools and reading teachers separated reading and writing into two separate lessons. Now it is not uncommon to have both reading and writing as part of the same lesson, at least some of the time. Literacy is defined as the ability to both read and write.

You can easily combine some of your lessons to include reading and writing. Chapter 6 will not only give you some suggestions on writing fundamentals like hand writing and spelling, but it will also encourage you to have children write some of their own reading material. Student-written stories can be a real creative outlet. Teachers can also write stories and develop experience charts that are interesting for their students to read because they are on topics of the students' own special interests.

Students of any age immediately see the usefulness of learning to write. There are many times in school, at work, and at home when writing is a valuable skill. There is also evidence that language uses - reading, writing, speaking and listening - are inter-related. A good teacher helps to develop them all. Step 6 will also give some suggestions on improving speaking and listening.

Trade Secrets

The following are a few tricks of the teaching trade that we have learned in the Reading Center at Rutgers University. Though they apply especially to children having problems learning to read (remedial readers), they also largely apply to normal students and adult learners in regular classrooms.

Success. Nothing motivates like success. In the Reading Center we say that a student must be successful with every lesson. If he is not, then we the tutors have given him the wrong lesson or have taught him in the wrong manner. We first seek a level where he can be successful. If he can't read a whole sentence in an easy book, we teach him just one word and say, "That's great! We are really getting somewhere now. Let's see if we can learn two whole words today." By building little success upon little success, you can soon change a sullen, reluctant truant into an eager learner.

Love. Students and adults who cannot read are rejected in many ways every day in school and in the world. They are set aside. They are different. They are failures. Not only have teachers failed to teach them, but teachers and society also constantly remind them of their problem just by giving the usual reading assignments in social studies or arithmetic, or by having written directions and newspapers around.

The successful reading teacher should remedy as many aspects of this situation as possible. If love is too strong a word, let's say that the teacher must care about the student and must use words and deeds to demonstrate that she cares.

Discipline. Just as love suggests a certain warmth and allowance for personality differences, so discipline suggests some structure for the teaching situation. A teacher can't love a child who is yelling in her face or who demands recess when she says it is time to study phonics.

We insist that a student get to lessons on time, have a minimum of absences, pay attention during lessons, and not be disruptive. Occasionally, after a few weeks of instruction, we have to offer some students a chance to stop reading lessons or settle down. We have never yet had the student decide to stop, but we would quite honestly let him stop if that is what he wanted. You can lead a horse to water, but you can't make him drink. The decision to learn must be the student's and not his parent's or the teacher's.

Interest. Most students are pretty poor actors when it comes to feigning interest. Learn to read the signs of lack of interest: losing the place in oral reading, daydreaming, fiddling with irrelevant objects, and so on. Discipline won't make boring lessons good lessons. The teacher must be skillful enough to present lessons that are easy enough to provide success, but difficult enough to provide challenge and growth.

Try to find reading materials that have a natural interest for the student. Turn some of your drill into competitive games, again keeping in mind that each student must experience some success. Students like to read about baseball, skin diving, mysteries, and so on, not stories about neat little children in short pants pulling wagons. Adults might find a lot of interest in reading want ads about good paying jobs or driver license manuals.

Rewards. Most people have their behavior modified by rewards. How long would most people go to work if they were not paid? Even when we do things without being paid, we get some kind of reward: the satisfaction of helping others, fun, companionship, or interest in doing something new. Sometimes the reward can be delayed -- most people go to school so that eventually they will earn more money. But all of us, especially children, like to have some immediate rewards. Hence, the teacher should use a wide variety of rewards. Here are a few suggestions:

* Praise a student at least once every lesson for something done well.
* Keep a progress chart of new words learned.
* Give gold stars or little trinkets for lessons completed or done especially well.
* See that the student has a chance to use his new skills in a meaningful situation.
* Have games that even poorer students can win occasionally.

17

Fluency. Good readers and good writers seem to do it almost effortlessly. They make it look easy. And how did they achieve that? The answer is by much practice. In fact, the experts in any skill, from playing tennis to playing the violin, often have much practice. It is, of course, quite possible to have some "natural ability" in any skill, including reading and writing, but most people need practice to develop a skill and even those with "natural ability" get better with practice.

You need to develop fluency, which can be defined as effortless reading with good comprehension, in your students. One way to do this is to give a lot of practice on an easy level before progressing to the next level of difficulty. Make sure the student has not only mastered a story (reads it without errors and has good comprehension) but has much additional practice on the story before progressing. Progressing too fast causes frustration, failure to learn and quitting (school drop outs or stopping lessons).

Now you've had a one-sentence answer, a one-paragraph answer, and a one-chapter answer to this question: How do you teach a child or an adult to read?

With this information, and the information given in the rest of this book, you can help any student learn to read better.

Good luck!

DETERMINE THE STUDENT'S READING ABILITY

Here you are, getting ready for your first session of teaching reading. What is your first step? It is to find out the present reading level of the student.

There are very few students who come to school, or adults in the civilized world, who read nothing. Almost everybody has some reading ability. The question is, "How much?"

Don't waste your time complaining that somebody else or some system should have taught your student how to read before this. Just find out how much your student can read right now, then get to work with lessons. Your student will thank you for the rest of his or her life when you are successful. Complaining never taught anybody anything.

How do you determine his present reading level? You test him with the Oral Reading Test.

Carefully read the following material that explains exactly how to use the Oral Reading Test. Then proceed with your first testing session.

There are other important methods of measuring the student's reading ability, but these will be discussed later.

Purpose of the Oral Reading Test

The purpose of this test is to aid instruction by determining the Independent Reading Level and the Instructional Reading Level of a child or an adult by having him read aloud several paragraphs.

Independent Reading Level. The Independent Reading Level is that difficulty level of reading material at which the student can read with relative ease and independence; in other words, with little or no help from the instructor. The student should be able to pronounce nearly all the words at this level. You can give your student reading material at this level for pleasure, practice and sustained silent reading.

Instructional Reading Level. The Instructional Reading level is that difficulty level of reading material at which reading instruction is most effective. The student should know most of the words, not all. Use this level for instruction, such as oral reading or silent reading, when you are around to help him with difficult words.

Frustration Reading Level. If reading instruction is given with material at too hard a level (that is, with too many unknown words), then the student's progress is not as rapid and symptoms of nervousness and dislike of reading may occur. Most of the time you should avoid getting your student reading material at his frustration level.

Now turn to the Test section at the end of this manual and glance over the Oral Reading Test on pages 118 to 127, and administer the test to your student.

SELECT THE RIGHT MATERIAL FOR THE STUDENT TO READ

Now you know how well your student can read. Because you have tested him with the Oral Reading Test, you know his Independent Reading Level and his Instructional Reading Level. Sometimes they are the same, but in any event, avoid the Frustration Level.

Your next step is to find reading materials on the right level for the student. With the Readability Graph (page 23) you can find the reading level of any book or story. From the List of Reading Materials (pages 26 and 29), you can find descriptions of instructional materials written on specific reading levels.

Matching

Matching and selecting the right reading material for your student is one of your most important jobs. If you give a student material that is too hard for him, the student will become bored with it and may stop reading, or his comprehension of the material will be poor. Even if he does struggle through it, it will take an excessive amount of time. On the other hand, if the student is given material that is too easy (which is not often the case), he may find it "babyish" and again become bored and stop reading.

The basic interest in the subject itself is, of course, an important factor. Given a very high interest, the student may work through more difficult material. But given only a normal amount of interest in the subject matter, if the material is too difficult, the student will stop reading. And most teachers would agree that it is very important for students to read, and read widely and frequently, if they are to be properly educated.

On the next page is a graph that will tell you the approximate difficulty level of any reading material. Use it in judging the grade level of reading material for your student. Try to match his reading ability (grade level obtained from the Oral Reading Test) with the grade level of the material. Remember, it is better to have the material a little too easy than a little too hard for reading instruction and especially for silent reading.

Informal Matching

If you don't want to use the Oral Reading Test and Readability Graph as aids in selecting material, you can match your student to a book by using the 1-error-in-20-words method shown in the box on page 10.

Some teachers and parents have philosophical objections to "tests". That's OK, there are many ways to teach reading. Obviously I don't think occasional curriculum-based tests do anything but make the lessons more effective. However there are plenty of other teaching suggestions in this book.

READABILITY GRAPH

Average number of syllables per 100 words

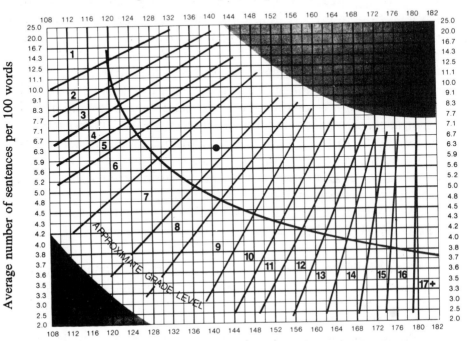

DIRECTIONS: Randomly select 3 one hundred word passages from a book or an article. Plot average number of syllables and average number of sentences per 100 words on graph to determine the grade level of the material. Choose more passages per book if great variability is observed and conclude that the book has uneven readability. Few books will fall in gray area but when they do grade level scores are invalid.

Count proper nouns, numerals and initializations as words. Count a syllable for each symbol. "1945" is 1 word and 4 syllables and "IRA" is 1 word and 3 syllables.

EXAMPLE:	SYLLABLES	SENTENCES
1st Hundred Words	124	6.6
2nd Hundred Words	141	5.5
3rd Hundred Words	158	6.8
AVERAGE	141	6.3

READABILITY 7th GRADE (see dot plotted on graph)

Interest Inventory

Most teachers find an interest inventory a good way of finding out about some of the students' interests. The following inventory can be used in part or in whole so that you can know more about your students' interests. If the student is deficient in writing skills, fill it out for him in an interview situation. Or you can just use the Interest Inventory as a suggestion list and ask the student some of the items.

Filling out the inventory should be a pleasant experience, not a chore. Tell the student that every question doesn't have to be answered. Don't penalize for spelling, but give help if needed. Most of these answers could use more space, so suggest the back of the sheet. In addition, almost any of the items on the inventory could be the suggested topic for a theme.

Finally, use the answers to the inventory items in selecting stories and reading materials for lessons.

You will find an Interest Inventory for children and one for adults on pages 27 and 28 at the end of this chapter.

List of Reading Materials

On page 29 at the end of this chapter, you will find a list of books. These are books frequently used in schools, but they can all be purchased from the publisher by anybody. Some public libraries have some of these books. You can use the stories in these books for oral reading or you can use them for silent reading. Teachers, school librarians, and public librarians can help you select interesting and easy reading material for your student.

Basal Readers

Children in school frequently learn to read from a set of books called a basal reading series. These series have stories and exercises for each grade level, usually 1 through 6. These books can be used to teach reading to either children or adults. But one serious problem in using them is that they are often childish for older students. For some students basal readers represent the kind of material that they failed on and hence they have bad associations. So you must decide whether you want to use some books from basal series or not. Basal readers can be used in part; in other words, you can just select a few stories in any book for use by your student. Sometimes public schools will lend or give you old copies of basal readers. Just ask the principal of a school near you. Also, many public libraries have copies of basal readers that they lend out free.

While traditional readers, like the old Scott Foresman Dick and Jane series, successfully taught millions of children how to read, they have come in for two types of criticism.

1. The stories lack high interest and good literary writing style.

2. The content of the stories was mostly about white, middle-class children from two parent homes, which doesn't match the home background of many of today's children.

But the newer basal readers overcome much of these criticisms. I think in tutoring situations, you can successfully use either old or new basal readers; most libraries have some of them. All basal readers are already graded (1st Grade difficulty, 2nd Grade .... etc.).

Trade Books

Trade books are the common children's story books found in book stores and libraries. Some are "classics" like *Little Red Riding Hood*, and some are just written last year and hope to become classics.

But be careful of this distinction:

Some books are meant to be read to children.

Some books are meant to be read by children.

For example, Dr. Seuss's *Cat in the Hat* is meant to be read by children because it uses simple words, repetition, and easier sentence construction, and is thus suitable for 1st Grade level. But Dr. Seuss's *How the Grinch Stole Christmas* is meant to be read to children of all ages, but is at the Frustration Reading Level for 1st Graders. At the end of this chapter is a lists of trade books suitable for instruction at different levels. Your public librarian, your school librarian, or other teachers can also be a big help in book selection.

There is a special type of children's trade book called "predictable" books or stories. These have a lot of repetition and are useful in teaching reading to children or even adults of any age. For an example of a predictable (repetitious) story, see the sample children's story *Busy, Busy Day* on page 141. For older children or adults the song *She'll Be Comin' Round The Mountain* on page 43 has a lot of repetition and can be used for reading instruction and fun.

Special and Unconventional Reading Materials

Good teachers and tutors often strive to make reading lessons more interesting by bringing to class special reading materials. Look over this list and maybe you will get some ideas for your students.

Drivers License Examination Booklet

Articles from a newspaper on the World Series, a local crime, a fashion tip, job want ads, a scientific discovery, a human interest story

A set of directions for assembling a toy or an appliance

Some jokes

Lyrics for a popular song

Short poems to be memorized

Danger signs and warnings

Local maps and **bus schedules**

Post Office forms

Student newspapers like *My Weekly Reader* or *Scholastic* papers -- used copies of these are sometimes given away free by public schools.

INTEREST INVENTORY FOR CHILDREN

Directions: To be filled out by the teacher or by the student with teacher assistance. This should be used in selecting interesting stories and reading materials. Most of these items can also be used as Story Starters or Titles for student themes.

My name is_____.

I am _____ years old.

Outside of school, the thing I like to do best is _____.

In school, the thing I like best is _____.

If I had a million dollars, I would _____.

When I grow up, I will _____.

I hate _____.

My favorite animal is _____.

The best sport is _____.

When nobody is around, I like to _____.

The person I like best is _____.

Next summer I hope to _____.

My father's work is _____.

My mother's work is _____.

When I grow up, I will be _____.

I like to collect _____.

The things I like to make are _____.

My favorite place to be is _____.

The best book I ever read was _____.

The best TV show is _____.

Favorite school subjects? _____.

INTEREST INVENTORY FOR ADULTS

Directions: To be filled out by the teacher or by the adult with teacher assistance.   This should be used in selecting interesting stories and reading materials.   Most of these items can also be used as Story Starters or Titles for student themes.

Name _____.

Occupation _____ Where _____.

Describe briefly what you really do _____.

What do you need to read on the job? _____.

What would you like to read for pleasure? _____.

Do you have a hobby? _____.

Sports interests? _____.

What would you do if you won a million dollars? __.

What kind of further schooling might you do? _____.

Have you ever read a book? (Which?) _____.

What do you do on vacation? _____.

Do you have any illness or health problems? _____.

Have you ever had your eyes or hearing checked?__.

What kind of work would you like to do in the future?_____.

If you moved, where would you like to go? _____.

What are your favorite kinds of food and drink? ___.

Any family problems? _____.

What is the best TV show? _____.

SOME FAVORITE CHILDREN'S TRADE BOOKS

Most of these are available in your library or local bookstore. Many of them even have paperback editions.

Charlotte's Web by E.B. White

The Berenstain Bears series, by Stan Berenstain and Janice Berenstain

The Ramona series, by Beverly Cleary

Superfudge, by Judy Blume

Tales of a Fourth Grade Nothing, by Judy Blume

The Little House series, by Laura I. Wilder

Where the Red Fern Grows, by Wilson Rawls

The Babysitters Club series, by Ann M. Martin

Cinderella, by Charles Perrault

The Velveteen Rabbit, by Margery Williams

Alexander and the Terrible, Horrible, No Good, Very Bad Day, by Judith Viorst

Ira Sleeps Over, by Bernard Waber

The Tale of Peter Rabbit, by Beatrix Potter

Winnie-the-Pooh, by A.A. Milne

The Laura Ingalls Wilder series, by Laura Ingalls Wilder

Little Women, by Louisa May Alcott

JOKES

Books never written:
    How To Do Gymnastics by Leo Tard
    Different Types of Sickness by Ty Foid
    Exercise Made Easy by Jim E. Quiptment
    Fast Cars by Otto Mobile

What do you call .....
    a cow with no legs? -- ground beef
    1000 rabbits moving backwards? -- a receding hare line
    a box lunch? -- square meal
    a skeleton that rings bells? -- a dead ringer

What is the laziest mountain in the world?
    Mount Ever Rest

How does a car feel after a long trip?
    Exhausted.

Why did Humpty Dumpty have a great fall?
    To make up for a crummy summer.

What do you get when you put four ducks in a small box?
    A box full of quackers

What do you get when you cross ....
    a pig and a pine tree? -- a pork-u-pine
    an owl and a goat? -- a hootenanny
    a midget and a computer? -- a short circuit

USEFUL SIGN WORDS

STOP	MEN	BUS
WALK	WOMEN	TAXI
DANGER	LADIES	AIRPORT
SCHOOL ZONE	GENTLEMEN	EXIT

Also see Important Signs on page 73, and you can make your own list of common useful signs and labels.

HAVE THE STUDENT READ ALOUD AND SILENTLY WITH COMPREHENSION

You have taken two important steps.

1. You have found your student's reading level.
2. You have matched it with the right reading material. Now what?

Now you must get your student to read and read and read. He should read orally with comprehension. He should read silently with comprehension.

In teaching reading comprehension, *variety* is the key word. Variety will add interest to your lessons. Variety will help to keep practice from becoming boring.

Variety in Subject Matter

The subject matter is one of the most obvious things that can be varied. It takes one approach to comprehend a set of directions on how to build a model airplane or how to bake a cake. It takes an entirely different approach to comprehend a story, and still another approach for a history lesson. All of these approaches involve reading, but you would want your student to read the history lesson more slowly and carefully than the story, and the directions even more carefully. What the author intends you to get from a story is not the same as what the author intends you to get from a history lesson or from a set of directions. You should point this out to the student. And the best way to point it out is not by lecturing, but by giving the student some simple questions following the reading.

Here are a few suggestions of different types of subject matter that you might select for comprehension drills and reading practice.

SUBJECT VARIETY SUGGESTIONS

Adventure stories-jungles, space, mountain climbing, foreign travel.
Biography-lives of heroes, famous people, minority leaders, movie stars.
Sports-baseball, auto racing, football, basketball (newspaper accounts of current sports events are sometimes especially useful with older students).
How to do it-get a job, repair a car, build a model, bake a cake, health and body building, beauty aids.
Romance and family situations-overcoming personal problems.
Strange and interesting-how people lived long ago, how their ancestors got there, causes of death, wars, floods, great inventions, animal stories, magic.

Variety in Length of Reading Selection

The length of the reading selection should be varied. In the beginning, getting your student to read one word or one sentence is often a feat. But even after learning to read a whole paragraph, your student should sometimes focus back on only one word or one sentence. As his ability advances, you will no doubt give him comprehension drills based on reading a paragraph or several paragraphs. This is a standard technique. As soon as possible, the student should read a whole story and then a whole book. Some students take real pride in having accomplished the feat of reading a whole book.

You can see the amount of variety you can add to comprehension drills by focusing on these different lengths of material:

LENGTH VARIETY SUGGESTIONS

A Word: Getting the meaning of one word is often called vocabulary building, but it is a kind of comprehension skill. Teachers should discuss and ask questions about one word sometimes. Also see Step 4.

A Phrase: Several words together often take on a meaning not contained in one word alone. The phrase "under the weather" doesn't have much to do with weather. See the list of idioms on page 42.

A Sentence: Sentences can be short and sweet with a simple noun-verb-object pattern, or they can be very complex with conditionals, subordinate clauses, and so on. Pick out some long and short sentences from the material you are using, discuss them, and ask comprehension questions about them.

LENGTH VARIETY SUGGESTIONS - Continued

A Paragraph: This is a traditional unit of teaching comprehension. It is good and should be used, but not exclusively. Be sure to use variety in questions discussed next.

A Chapter or Story: In many books, groups of paragraphs form a larger unit. Teach your students to read larger units. Show that sometimes you have to see several paragraphs in relation to each other to get meaning. Ask questions that can only be answered by reading many paragraphs or the whole story.

A Book: Even younger students like long stories sometimes. Guide them into reading easy whole books, then slightly harder ones.

Variety in Type of Questions

The type of questions can be very important in teaching comprehension. The easiest type of question to ask is the "specific detail" question such as "What was the color of the boy's hair?" It is good to get the facts straight, but here are some more interesting types of questions that you can use. Avoid questions that can be answered "yes" or "no" or with a one word answer.

QUESTION TYPE VARIETY

Time Sequence: What happened first?
What happened next?
What happened after ...?
When did the characters ...?

Setting: Where does this story take place: at home, in the park, in the city, in the country? (specific)
Where does this story take place: out West, in New York, in America, in Europe, in Outer Space? (general)
In what period of time does this story take place: in a morning, a day, a year?
In what period of history does this story take place: modern day, during World War II, in the Middle Ages, in prehistoric times?
What do you know about that period from other things you have read?
What was the weather like? Did it have anything to do with how the characters felt or with what happened?

Summary: Restate the paragraph or story in your own words.

QUESTION TYPE VARIETY -- Continued

Main Idea: What is this story (article) mainly about?
What point is the writer making?
What is the main idea of paragraph three? Is the main idea stated in a sentence in the paragraph?
What is the main idea of the whole story (article)?
Why did the writer choose this title for the story?
Can you think of a better title?

Character Traits: What does the hero look like?
What kind of person do you think he is? Why? Is the hero happy? Honest? Why?

(Note: These questions often require the student to do some creative interpreting, since they may not be answered directly in the story.)

Conclusions: How do you think the writer feels about ... ? Why?
What can you conclude from this story about ... ? Why?
Which of the following is probably true: ... ? Why?
When the hero said, " ......", how do you think he felt? Or, did he really mean something else?
Why do you think so?
What might happen next? (if story were to continue)

QUESTION TYPE VARIETY -- Continued

(Note: Keep in mind that a conclusion must be supported by facts in the story. The student in response to "Why?" should support his answer by referring to the story.)

Newspaper
Questions: Who? What? Why? When? Where? How?

Comparison: Is this better than the last story you read?
Which story was writted longer ago?
Was anything about the two heroes the same? Different?
What else do you know about people or event like this?

By using a variety of question types, you can keep the student interested and at the same time cover a wide range of comprehension skills.   Don't ask questions that require comprehension skills that are above the level of your student. Ask questions that the student can often answer successfully.

Variety in Difficulty of Level of Material

The difficulty level of the material should be varied.   Of course, you want to give a lot of practice on easy material because it helps the reader feel successful, and this is very important. However, you do need to move the pupil ahead to harder material. So try out comprehension drills first on easy material, then on slightly harder material.   If the student experiences failure or frustration, return to the easy material for a while.

Attempting to vary the difficulty level can add interest. Sometimes students will enjoy doing a comprehension drill or reading a book that is very simple for them.   But sometimes they feel absolutely triumphant about mastering harder material.

Variety in Response

The type of response that you ask a student to make to a question is very important and can have some variety. Perhaps the easiest type of question requires some memory or "recall" as the psychologists like to call it. A question is asked and the student gives an answer. The questions or directions may specify whether a long answer (sentence or several sentences) is required, or a short answer (word or phrase) is required.

Another type of answer variation is between written and oral answers. Sometimes the teacher will want the student to answer with his pencil and sometimes by speaking. The same type of variation also applies to the kind of reading done; that is, the reading may be oral or silent. Thus, a teacher may have oral questions following silent reading one day and silently read questions and written responses following oral reading of the passage on the next day.

Multiple choice questions are often used in commercially prepared comprehension drills. Not only is this type of question good for comprehension drills, but it is frequently the kind of question used in testing the student's knowledge in a wide variety of situations. Hence, the student should have some practice in handling this type of question. Occasionally students enjoy making up multiple-choice questions for each other on some reading material. A similar type of choice question, but limited to two choices, is the True/False type of question.

Cloze is another type of comprehension drill question. It is also sometimes called the sentence completion technique. To make cloze questions is very simple. Just knock out a word - any word - in a sentence and see if the student can fill it in. The simplest type of cloze drill is mechanical deletion, where you might just leave out every 10th word. More meaningful exercises might have more meaningful deletions, such as only subject matter words (noun, adjective, verb or adverb). Do not delete more often than every 10th word or else the student will get a little frustrated with the task. Some students, particularly students for whom English is a second language, need drills on language usage. For these students, cloze techniques which knock out structure words (anything not a subject word) are very interesting as well as beneficial. For example, in making a structure word cloze drill, you might have a paragraph like this:

Rosa went to ____ store for her mother.
"Are you the new girl?" asked the man ____ the store.

The student's task is to fill in the missing word. Select passages that are on the easy-reading side for the student.

You can also get into some interesting discussions about the exact word versus the kind of word that can be put into the blank space.

Don't use this type of drill too much. It is excellent, but overused it becomes a bore. So stick to the main idea of this chapter: variety.

Student generated questions are sometimes fun. Simply ask your student to make up his own questions for a paragraph or a story. The teacher then must answer the student's questions and discuss the answers. If you have two or more students, they can make up questions for each other. Be sure to reward the student making up the questions by much praise like, "That's a fine question; it really made me think." By praising just the good questions, you can get a better set of questions the next time you do this type of lesson.

Retelling the story is a simple but very effective comprehension type of lesson. Simply ask the student to retell the story in his own words after he has read it silently. If the student cannot tell you the story, there is a good chance he has not understood it. If this happens, just ask him to read the story again a little more carefully because you are going to ask him to tell you all about it. This will also give you the opportunity to teach comprehension by saying, "If there is any part that you do not understand, just ask me about it." Incidentally, the retelling can be either oral or written. If the student has sufficient writing skills, ask him to write a short version of the story in his own words. You can also help him with his writing skills.

If the student is bilingual and you are bilingual, for example if you both speak Spanish, ask the student to read the story in English but tell you about it in Spanish - this is an excellent comprehension check.

```
┌─────────────────────────────────────────────┐
│          RESPONSE VARIETY SUMMARY            │
│                                              │
│  1. Vary answer length (ex. long, short)     │
│                                              │
│  2. Multiple choice or True/False            │
│                                              │
│  3. Cloze - fill in missing word(s)          │
│                                              │
│  4. Student makes up questions               │
│                                              │
│  5. Retelling or summarizing                 │
│                                              │
└─────────────────────────────────────────────┘
```

Standardized Silent Reading Tests

Schools often give reading tests and the scores are available to parents, teachers and tutors.

The names of some important reading achievement tests are: California Reading Test, Stanford, SRA, Metropolitan, and Iowa.

It is important to know a little bit about silent reading tests. Formal or standardized tests tell you approximately what grade level of reading ability the student has achieved. These tests are another important measure (along with the oral tests) of the student's reading ability. They are useful for measuring progress over the period of a year or more, and they are useful in helping you select books and stories on the proper difficulty level.

Not every section of a standardized silent reading test is equally valuable. The most important part, or the part that you should pay the most careful attention to, is the part which measures paragraph comprehension. This section is sometimes called Comprehension or Reading Interpretations. But whatever it is called, it consists of asking the student to read one or several paragraphs and then to answer one or more questions about what he has just read.

A Reading Comprehension Test You Can Use

You may wish to test your student's reading comprehension. It is not required, but it does give you some more information about your student's reading ability.

At the end of this manual on pages 128 through 139 are two Reading Comprehension Tests that you can use to measure the reading comprehension ability of an individual student or of a group. Test A is at approximately the nine-year-old or third grade level; Test B is at approximately the thirteen-year-old or seventh grade level. However, either test may be used with students of any age, including adults, to get some idea of reading comprehension ability.

The items originated with the National Assessment of Educational Progress, which administered each item all across the United States. Hence you can compare your student with average third graders or average seventh graders.

The items cover a variety of reading comprehension skills. Although you cannot conclude that a student is weak in an area based on one item alone, the items do indicate something about the student's abilities and do give you some suggestions for types of reading comprehension questions to use in drills.

Do not use the test items for teaching. You should not tell the student which items he got right or wrong, nor should you "go over" the test with the student. By doing so, you invalidate the use of the test for that student in the future. If you do not go over the test items (tell the student which item is wrong or right), you can use exactly the same test at a later time to show progress in reading ability.

The List of Reading Materials in Step 2 of this manual indicates materials that you can use to teach comprehension, or you can make up your own comprehension questions similar to those in the test using other materials. Since the question types discussed in this Step on the preceding pages will also guide you in writing your own comprehension questions, don't use the test for teaching.

IDIOMATIC EXPRESSIONS

Sometimes a student can't understand a phrase or a sentence because an idiomatic expression is used. An idiomatic expression is a group of words that has a meaning different from what those words usually mean or different from the meaning of the words used in another way. For example, "It is raining cats and dogs" doesn't usually mean that cats are coming down from the sky.

Some of these can be pictured humorously and many have to be explained to students for whom English is a second language.

Time flies.
She's over the hill.
We don't see eye to eye.
Go fly a kite.
He has a green thumb.
You put your foot in your mouth.
Go jump in the lake.
Keep a straight face.
Throw your weight around.
Eat your words.
He really blew up.
Pull the wool over her eyes.
Keep the wolf from the door.
He fell for her.
She hit the roof.
It brought down the house.
Hit the books.
She turned a cold shoulder to me.
I look up to him.
You see through him.
That hit the nail on the head.
Cut it out.
Turn over a new leaf.

SONGS

Song lyrics are a fun and useful thing to read. They help to teach reading because they often have much repetition and the student can memorize them and hence "read" them with ease and success. But just in case you want to make sure real reading is taking place, take some words out of the song and write them in isolation on a piece of paper or a chalkboard or just point to random words.

She'll Be Comin' Round the Mountain

She'll be comin' round the mountain when she comes.
She'll be comin' round the mountain when she comes.
She'll be comin' round the mountain,
She'll be comin' round the mountain,
She'll be comin' round the mountain when she comes.

2. She'll be drivin' six white horses when she comes. (etc.)

3. Oh, we'll all go out to meet her when she comes. (etc.)

4. Oh, we'll kill the old red rooster when she comes. (etc.)

Clementine

In a cavern, in a canyon, excavating for a mine,
Dwelt a miner, forty-niner, and his daughter Clementine.

Chorus:

Oh my darling, oh my darling, oh my darling, Clementine!
Thou art lost and gone forever. Dreadful sorry, Clementine.

2. Light she was and like a fairy,
And her shoes were number nine,
Herring boxes without topses,
Sandals were for Clementine. *Chorus*

SONGS -- Continued

3. Drove she ducklings to the water,
   Ev'ry morning just at nine,
   Hit her foot against a splinter,
   Fell into the foaming brine. *Chorus*

4. Ruby lips above the water,
   Blowing bubbles soft and fine,
   But, alas, I was no swimmer,
   So I lost my Clementine. *Chorus*

5. How I missed her! How I missed her,
   How I missed my Clementine.
   But I kissed her little sister,
   I forgot my Clementine. *Chorus*

Jingle Bells

Dashing through the snow, in a one horse open sleigh,
And o'er the fields we go, laughing all the way.
The bells on bob tail ring. They're making spirits bright,
What fun it is to ride and sing a sleighing song tonight!

Chorus:

Jingle bells! Jingle bells! Jingle all the way!
Oh what fun it is to ride in a one horse open sleigh. (repeat)

2. A day or so ago,
   I thought I'd take a ride,
   And soon Miss Fannie Bright
   Was seated by my side.
   The horse was lean and lank,
   Misfortune seemed his lot,
   He got into a drifted bank,
   And we? We got upsot! *Chorus*

SONGS -- Continued

3. Now the ground is white,
   Go it while you're young,
   Take the girls tonight,
   And sing this sleighing song.
   Just get a bob-tailed nag,
   Two-forty for his speed,
   Then hitch him to an open sleigh,
   And crack! You'll take the lead. *Chorus*

All libraries have song books if you want more songs for reading lessons. These came from a book called "Best Loved Songs of the American People" by Denes Agay.

READING IDEA

Get a library card!
Check out a new book every week!
Read a bit of the new book in the library before you bring it home.

TEACH VOCABULARY

Teaching vocabulary for reading teachers is usually divided into two quite different levels. Beginning readers need to master (1) a <u>basic sight vocabulary</u> of common words and more advanced readers need (2) <u>vocabulary improvement</u>, which means learning the meaning of new words.

Beginning readers, who for now we will define as anybody, child or adult, whose ability ranges from none to upper 3rd grade, need to master a high frequency vocabulary such as the Instant Words that are given at the end of this section. For example, they need to be able to read the first 300 Instant Words "instantly" without a moment's hesitation because these 300 words make up 65% of all written material. That's right, over half of every newspaper article, every textbook, every children's story, every novel, is composed of just these 300 words! These are words that come up over and over again – words like "the", "of", and "and". You can hardly write any sentence without using several of the first 300 Instant Words. And you certainly can't concentrate on comprehension if you are trying to figure out "their".

Another problem is that some of these often used words do not follow regular phonics rules very well. For example, how do you sound out "of" or "said"? The answer is that beginning readers need to learn these words as "sight words".

The first part of this Chapter will show you how to test your student to find out which of the Instant Words he knows and then it will present some methods for teaching them. The second part of this Chapter will discuss some vocabulary improvement techniques for students who have better than 3rd grade reading ability.

Testing the Instant Words

One of the important tools in every remedial teacher's "bag of tricks" should be a list of the most frequently used words in reading. Children and adults who are just learning or who have failed to learn to read properly from regular instruction frequently have a very spotty reading vocabulary. They know some relatively uncommon words, while they do not know some of the words that appear most frequently.

Most basic reading textbooks have their own graded list built into the series. But perhaps your student has followed no basic text series or else has learned only part of the list. If so, you must "find out where the learner is".

To do this with an individual student is easy. Use the Instant Word Test (page 64) or simply ask him to read aloud from each column of the Instant Words (pages 58 to 63). Then stop and teach him the words he doesn't know.

If you have to work with groups, a way of diagnosing word knowledge for beginning readers is to make a recognition test. Ditto a group of Instant Words, four words per line; number the lines. Give each student a sheet with the words on it and then say, "On line 1 put an 'X' on the word 'you', line 2 put an 'X' on the word 'that'", and so on.

By correcting the tests, you can easily sort the pupils into ability and groups. Incidentally, save the tests and use them for the children to study from or review the words.

If you don't want to use this survey test, just have your student read every word on the Instant Word Charts - but not all at once; perhaps a column or part of a column at each lesson, until you have accumulated enough unknown words.

Teaching the Instant Words

Since a high percentage of all reading material is composed of relatively few words, learning to read would appear to be a task which is ridiculously easy: If 300 words will do such a large percentage of the job, why not begin with just these words, teach them quickly, and get it over with at once? The trouble is that it is not easy.

Experience has shown that, normally, mastery of the first 300 Instant Words (or of any basic vocabulary list of this size for that matter) could be expected to take nearly three years for primary children. An average student, in an average school situation, learns most of the first one hundred words toward the end of the first year. The second hundred words are added during the second year. It is not until some time in the third year that all 300 words are really mastered and used as a part of the student's own reading vocabulary. This is not to deny that second and third graders can "read" many more words than the 300 Instant Words. They can also read many proper nouns and a spattering of subject words related to the type of material that they have been exposed to.

One can expect to decrease the learning time required in the case of older students, illiterate adults and students in upper elementary and secondary remedial reading classes. Still, their learning of the first 300 Instant Words is found to parallel closely their attained reading ability level. For example, a person who can just manage to read upper second grade material barely knows most of the first two hundred Instant Words.

A list of 600 Instant Words are given at the end of this Chapter. Make sure that your student knows most of the first 300 Instant Words "instantly" before proceeding to teach the second 300 Instant Words. The second 300 Instant Words are for reading and spelling lessons with students of 4th and 5th grade ability.

Methods for teaching the Instant Words vary with the teacher, the pupil, and the educational situation. We say any method that works is a good method.

We use card games, easy reading practice, flash cards, and spelling lessons augmented by lavish praise, stern talks, competition, or a play-therapy climate. The pupil learns to read words in books, on flash cards, in his own compositions, or off wall charts.

We teach him alone and in large groups, in the classroom and out under the trees. But all the while we are constantly telling him three things by word and deed: (1) We care about him. (2) We want him to read. (3) These Instant Words are important. Here are some specific methods.

Note that the Instant Words are in groups of five. This is to remind you that you shouldn't try to teach too many words at once. Some students can learn only 2 or 3 words per week and others can gobble down 20. Both need frequent review.

Easy Reading Practice. Easy reading practice is one of the best ways of teaching the Instant Words. For a student who can read on the second grade level (whether with help or hesitatingly), "easy reading" is reading first grade level materials. Betts gives an excellent definition of easy reading material - printed matter in which a student can pronounce 99 percent of the words. Another Betts rule-of-thumb is that when the student averages fewer than one mistake for every 20 words, the material is "easy" for him. Easy reading practice is especially beneficial because the material is certain to contain the Instant Words, and a student who barely knows these words gets practice in recognizing them. Easy reading practice helps a student to learn to apply context clues. Each reading gives the student a feeling of success, and encourages him to try to learn more.

Easy reading then is reading that is a grade or two below where the student "can" read. If a student can read at 6th grade level, easy reading is at the 4th or 5th grade level. It is no accident that most popular novels are written at about the 8th grade difficulty level while most book buyers are at least high school graduates.

Flash Cards. Many teachers, tutors and parents use flash cards to help teach sight word reading. A flash card is simply a card with a word written on it. The word is written in bold print using a marker or dark crayon. Usually the print is in lower case letters, like most of the words in this book.

she

said

A traditional way to teach using flash cards is to take a small number of words like 5 Instant Words. Tell the student each word and discuss it a little, perhaps using it in an oral sentence. Next, mix up the cards and "flash" them to the student while the student tries to quickly call out the word. If he misses, tell him the word (don't use phonics at this point). Mix up the words and flash them to the student again. After the student knows all the words, put them away and at the next lesson review them by flashing the cards and helping the student with any words missed.

One of the nice things about flash cards is that they make great review lessons, and students often require much review of these words. Just because they have mastered the list one day, don't be surprised if they don't remember all the words next week. This is why review and more practice are needed. Incidentally, don't blame the student for forgetting. Instead, praise him for any words he remembers and patiently teach the missed words. Every human being needs repetition when learning new words. Perhaps you need some repetitions in learning people's names or in learning new words connected with your business or in a new subject you are studying.

Another thing you can do with flash cards is to display them for referral at other times in the day. Teachers might line them up on the chalkboard, mothers might stick them on the refrigerator, and tutors might hand a small stack to the student to take home for practice.

Flash cards can also be used as Sentence Builders. Put 2 or 3 or more flash cards in order so that they make a phrase or a sentence. You can make some interesting sentences using rebuses. A rebus is simply a picture used instead of a word, for example:

The **hit the**

Read this as "The boy hit the dog."

We frequently use flash cards with small groups. The teacher flashes the word as quickly as possible. The student who says the word first gets to hold the card. The point of the game is to see who gets the most cards. Give each student a turn at recognizing the word; when he misses, the next student gets the turn.

A student sometimes works alone with a small pack of flash cards, separating them into two piles - (1) the cards he knows, and

(2) those he does not know. When he is finished, the teacher or a superior student checks up on the "know" pile and then helps him with the "don't know" pile.

You can make your own flash cards on blank calling cards (obtained from a printer), on 3 x 5 cards, or on scraps of paper. You can copy the whole list or you can make cards for just the words the student misses from reading down the list. Remember - don't try to teach too many words at once. Keep the student's success rate high.

Bingo Game. Bingo is an excellent game for teaching Instant Words to large groups, but it is equally useful for small groups or even a single student. Twenty-five words can be placed on a card (five rows and five columns) in random order, with a card each for as many students as are playing. The teacher calls off the words in random order, or may take the precaution of drawing the word cards out of a hat. Markers can be small squares of cardboard, bottle caps, beans, or anything handy. The first student to complete a row or column or diagonal line wins.

Oftentimes, even though there has been a winner, the students like to play on until the board is filled, so that every word is covered. If played until the board is filled, the teacher can sometimes spot poor readers by the number of uncovered words. In a teaching situation where some of the students do not know all the words, excellent instruction can ensue by having the teacher show the card or write the word on the board after saying it. This gives poor readers an equal chance at winning, which is always desirable.

Note that by making 5 rows and 5 columns, one set of 25 Instant Words will fit on a card. For young children or beginning readers, you can make bingo cards with just 9 words (3 rows and 3 columns).

Remember that each player must have a card with the same words, but arranged in a different order.

SAMPLE BINGO CARD

the	of	it	with	at
a	can	on	are	this
is	will	you	to	and
your	that	we	as	but
be	in	not	for	have

Pairs Game. Another game played with great success is called Pairs. Pairs is played like Rummy or Fish, except that only 2 cards are needed to make a book or pair. Two to five persons may play. Five cards are dealt to each player, and the remainder of the deck is placed in the center of the table.

The object of the game is to get as many pairs as possible. There are only two cards alike in each deck.

The player to the right of the dealer may ask any single other player if he has a specific card. For example, "Do you have 'and'?" The player asking must hold the mate (in the example, the "and" card) in his hand. The player who is asked must give up the card if he holds it. If the first player does not get the card he asks for, he should draw one card from the pile. Then the next player has a turn at asking for a card.

If the player succeeds in getting the card he asked for, either from another player or from the pile, he gets another turn. As soon as the player gets a pair, he puts the pair down in front of him. The player with the most pairs at the end of the game wins.

If the player <u>doing the asking</u> does not know how to read the word on the card, he may show the card and ask any of the other players or anyone present.

If the player <u>who is asked</u> for a card does not know how to read that word or is unsure of himself, the best thing to do is ask to see the card of the player requesting the card or ask a non-playing person who can read to look at his hand.

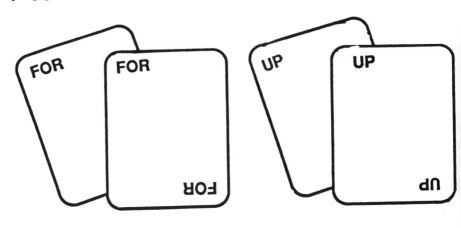

Make two cards for each word in a Pairs game deck.

The students should know some but not all the words used in a particular deck. They should have help in playing until they know almost all the words and can get along by themselves. They can usually accomplish this quite rapidly as the game is highly motivating. The students should play the game on several different occasions until they can call out all the words instantly. They should then move to the next harder deck. Reviewing easier decks is also recommended.

Make the card decks with groups of 25 Instant Words; two cards for each word makes a 50-card deck. Your student can help you make the decks. Make the decks for the level of words your student needs to learn.

Once in a while, it is good to review easy words already mastered, just for fun. But, generally, instructional games should follow the same rules as those set up for the selection of instructional reading material, i.e., not too easy, and not too hard.

Concentration.   The Pairs decks can also be used to play a Concentration game. Take a deck of 50 cards and place them face down spread out over a table in mixed up order. One to 4 players can play. Each player turns over 2 cards. If they are a pair, he keeps them and if they are not a pair, then they must be put back in exactly the same place, face down. The trick of the game is to remember the location of cards so one can make a pair with each 2 cards turned up. From a reading instruction standpoint, the student must read aloud each card turned over. If he doesn't know how to read the card, another player can tell him.

Spelling.   The Instant Words may be used for spelling lessons, particularly words which the students have trouble learning to read.   But for student writing the Instant Words are just as important as they are for reading.   You can't write any story without using some of the Instant Words. A typical spelling lesson has these elements:

1. The student is shown the words to be learned on a chalkboard, on flash cards, or on a piece of paper. He is asked to read them aloud and sometimes use them in sentences orally so you are sure that he knows how to pronounce them and knows the meaning of them.

2. The student may copy the words or write them in a sentence.

3. The student is given a trial test, which means the teacher says the word and the student tries to write it.

4. The student's trial test is corrected and each incorrect letter or missing letter is circled or added.

5. The student studies the errors and practices writing the words correctly.

6. The final spelling test is given. Any words containing mistakes are added to next week's spelling list.

Don't give too many words in a spelling lesson. For example, 5 to 10 words for a beginner (1st grade level) and 20 words for grade levels 3 to 6.

For more information on teaching spelling and 195 weekly spelling lessons covering difficulty levels grades 1-6, see the *Spelling Book* published by Laguna Beach Educational Books.

Picture Nouns. Picture nouns are a one hundred word list at the end of this Chapter intended to supplement the Instant Words. They are words that can easily be pictured and they are words that students need when writing stories. The Instant Words do not have too many "subject words": those words that tell about the content.

car

boat

The Picture Nouns can be taught along with the Instant Words, a group of 5 at a time. They are particularly useful in using flash cards as Sentence Builders and the picture side of the card can be used as a rebus (picture for a word in a sentence).

Picture Nouns can also be used in "thinking skills". Take 2 or more groups of 5 Picture Nouns, mix them up, and have the student sort them into piles that belong together. It makes the student "think" and it gives him practice reading words.

The Picture Nouns can also be used in self-teaching lessons. Give the student a stack of cards with the word side up. The student tries to read the word, and if he can't, he turns the card over to look at the picture.

Most of the games and techniques used in teaching the Instant Words can also be used with the Picture Nouns.

Vocabulary Building

The term "Vocabulary Building" is used mostly for more mature reading students, such as those students of any age who are reading better than third grade difficulty level. Basically these are students who recognize instantly most of the first 300 Instant Words and who have a fair grasp of basic phonics skills.

Pay Attention. The first rule in vocabulary building is <u>when you encounter a new word while reading, pause and pay attention to it</u>. See if you can get the meaning of the word from the way it is used in the sentence. If you can't, ask someone or "ask" the dictionary.

Direct Instruction. A second major method of new vocabulary learning is direct instruction for new words. Some teachers and families put up a new word a day on the chalkboard, a bulletin board, or a card on the table, and discuss it briefly. For example, you might put up "inclement" on a rainy day, or "torrid" on a hot day. Maybe the new word comes from hearing it used on TV or in a newspaper, like "seismograph" when describing earthquakes or "coup" when reporting revolutions.

Prefixes and Roots. Learning to use word prefixes and roots is also a good way to expand vocabulary. Even little children know that "un" in front of a word changes its meaning, as in "unhappy" and they can extend this to learning the meaning of "unable". The same idea applies to word roots. For example, "tele" means "far", so "television" means vision or seeing something that is far away. This root is also seen in "telescope", "telegram", etc. and helps to explain the meaning of those words.

A list of some common prefixes and roots can be found at the end of this Chapter in case you need some to start teaching in this manner. Also, most large dictionaries give the root meaning of many words and that can help you learn the meaning of that word and other words that use that root.

Use New Words. Finally, you should keep in mind that learning new words is a life-long task. Every time you start to learn a new subject or read a new book, you will encounter new words to be learned. Welcome the task and enjoy it. It will also help to learn new words if you try to use them in speech and writing. Encourage your student to try using any new word. Praise him for its use even if it is mispronounced or misspelled. It is through use that words become a permanent part of one's vocabulary.

VOCABULARY BUILDING

To review some of these points on vocabulary building:

1. Pay attention to new words.
2. Ask someone their meaning.
3. Look them up in a dictionary.
4. Learn a new word a day.
5. Study prefixes and roots.
6. Use new words often.

---

600 INSTANT WORDS

These are the most often used words in reading and writing. The first 100 words are listed in order of frequency in Columns 1 through 4. Make sure your student knows most of these before teaching the second 100. Teach only a few at a time to keep the success rate high. Use these words for flash cards, games, spelling lessons, or just reading down the column. These high frequency words are also called "sight words" because they must be recognized instantly on sight for reading fluency.

Column 1 Words 1-25	Column 2 Words 26-50	Column 3 Words 51-75	Column 4 Words 76-100
the	or	will	number
of	one	up	no
and	had	other	way
a	by	about	could
to	words	out	people
in	but	many	my
is	not	then	than
you	what	them	first
that	all	these	water
it	were	so	been
he	we	some	called
was	when	her	who
for	your	would	oil
on	can	make	sit
are	said	like	now
as	there	him	find
with	use	into	long
his	an	time	down
they	each	has	day
I	which	look	did
at	she	two	get
be	do	more	come
this	how	write	made
have	their	go	may
from	if	see	part

INSTANT WORDS -- Continued
The Second Hundred Instant Words

Column 5 Words 101-125	Column 6 Words 126-150	Column 7 Words 151-175	Column 8 Words 176-200
over	say	set	try
new	great	put	kind
sound	where	end	hand
take	help	does	picture
only	through	another	again
little	much	well	change
work	before	large	off
know	line	must	play
place	right	big	spell
years	too	even	air
live	means	such	away
me	old	because	animals
back	any	turned	house
give	same	here	point
most	tell	why	page
very	boy	asked	letters
after	following	went	mother
things	came	men	answer
our	want	read	found
just	show	need	study
name	also	land	still
good	around	different	learn
sentence	form	home	should
man	three	us	American
think	small	move	world

INSTANT WORDS -- Continued
The Third Hundred Instant Words

Column 9 Words 201-225	Column 10 Words 226-250	Column 11 Words 251-275	Column 12 Words 276-300
high	saw	important	miss
every	left	until	idea
near	don't	children	enough
add	few	side	eat
food	while	feet	face
between	along	car	watch
own	might	miles	far
below	close	night	Indians
country	something	walked	really
plants	seemed	white	almost
last	next	sea	let
school	hard	began	above
father	open	grow	girl
keep	example	took	sometimes
trees	beginning	river	mountains
never	life	four	cut
started	always	carry	young
city	those	state	talk
earth	both	once	soon
eyes	paper	book	list
light	together	hear	song
thought	got	stop	being
head	group	without	leave
under	often	second	family
story	run	later	it's

INSTANT WORDS -- Continued
The Fourth Hundred Instant Words

Column 13 Words 301-325	Column 14 Words 326-350	Column 15 Words 351-375	Column 16 Words 376-400
body	order	listen	farm
music	red	wind	pulled
color	door	rock	draw
stand	sure	space	voice
sun	become	covered	seen
questions	top	fast	cold
fish	ship	several	cried
area	across	hold	plan
mark	today	himself	notice
dog	during	toward	south
horse	short	five	sing
birds	better	step	war
problem	best	morning	ground
complete	however	passed	fall
room	low	vowel	king
knew	hours	true	town
since	black	hundred	I'll
ever	products	against	unit
piece	happened	pattern	figure
told	whole	numeral	certain
usually	measure	table	field
didn't	remember	north	travel
friends	early	slowly	wood
easy	waves	money	fire
heard	reached	map	upon

INSTANT WORDS -- Continued
The Fifth Hundred Instant Words

Column 17 Words 401-425	Column 18 Words 426-450	Column 19 Words 451-475	Column 20 Words 476-500
done	decided	plane	filled
English	contain	system	heat
road	course	behind	full
half	surface	ran	hot
ten	produce	round	check
fly	building	boat	object
gave	ocean	game	am
box	class	force	rule
finally	note	brought	among
wait	nothing	understand	noun
correct	rest	warm	power
oh	carefully	common	cannot
quickly	scientists	bring	able
person	inside	explain	six
became	wheels	dry	size
shown	stay	though	dark
minutes	green	language	ball
strong	known	shape	material
verb	island	deep	special
stars	week	thousands	heavy
front	less	yes	fine
feel	machine	clear	pair
fact	base	equation	circle
inches	ago	yet	include
street	stood	govern-ment	built

INSTANT WORDS -- Continued
The Sixth Hundred Instant Words

Column 21 Words 501-525	Column 22 Words 526-550	Column 23 Words 551-575	Column 24 Words 576-600
can't	picked	legs	beside
matter	simple	sat	gone
square	cells	main	sky
syllables	paint	winter	glass
perhaps	mind	wide	million
bill	love	written	west
felt	cause	length	lay
suddenly	rain	reason	weather
test	exercise	kept	root
direction	eggs	interest	instru- ments
center	train	arms	meet
farmers	blue	brother	third
ready	wish	race	months
anything	drop	present	paragraph
divided	developed	beautiful	raised
general	window	store	represent
energy	difference	job	soft
subject	distance	edge	whether
Europe	heart	past	clothes
moon	sit	sign	flowers
region	sum	record	shall
return	summer	finished	teacher
believe	wall	discovered	held
dance	forest	wild	describe
members	probably	happy	drive

In case you want more Instant Words for reading or spelling lessons, the entire list of 3000 Instant Words can be found in the Spelling Book, Words Most Needed Plus Phonics for Grades 1-6, which is available from Phoenix Learning Resources, 468 Park Avenue South, New York, NY 10016 (800-221-1274).

DIRECTIONS FOR THE INSTANT WORD TEST

The Instant Word Test is located on the next page. Ask the pupil to read each word aloud slowly. The examiner should use a copy of the Instant Word Test for scoring. Place a "C" next to each word read correctly. Although you should allow for regional dialect differences, accept only proper pronunciations. Do not give any aid. If a pupil does not know a word, tell him to go on to the next word after five seconds.

Discontinue when the student misses five words, not necessarily in consecutive order. Find the last correct word before the fifth error, and multiply its position number by 15. This will give you the student's approximate instructional placement.

Because it is not standardized, the test does not yield a grade level score, but it can be used to determine where to begin working with a student on the first 600 Instant Words. Do not use this test for teaching; use the complete list of 600 Instant Words, which is just before this page and starts on page 58.

INSTANT WORD TEST

Student's Name _____

Examiner _____

Date _____Class _____

Test for the First 300 Words
(approximately every 15th
word in the First 300 Words)

Test for the Second 300 Words
(approximately every 15th
word in the Second 300 Words)

1. are	**21.** room
2. but	**22.** become
3. which	**23.** whole
4. so	**24.** toward
5. see	**25.** map
6. now	**26.** king
7. only	**27.** certain
8. just	**28.** stars
9. too	**29.** nothing
10. small	**30.** stood
11. why	**31.** bring
12. again	**32.** check
13. study	**33.** heavy
14. last	**34.** direction
15. story	**35.** picked
16. beginning	**36.** window
17. feet	**37.** wide
18. book	**38.** sign
19. almost	**39.** root
20. family	**40.** describe

Directions: Student reads aloud from one copy and examiner marks another copy. Stop after the student misses any five words. Do not help the student. If the student makes an error or hesitates 5 seconds, say, "Try the next word". Scoring:

(   ) Position number of last correct word before the fifth word missed.

X   15

(   ) Approximate placement on the First 600 Instant Words.

For example, if the last correct word was 10, then 10 x 15 = 150. So start teaching the Instant Words with word 151 in Column 7.

100 PICTURE NOUNS

These words are intended to supplement the first 300 Instant Words for use in beginning or remedial reading instruction. These words can be made into flash cards with the word on one side only or cards with the word on one side and the picture on the other.

front   back

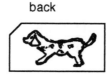

dog

1. People
   boy
   girl
   man
   woman
   baby

2. Toys
   ball
   doll
   train
   game
   toy

3. Numbers 1-5
   one
   two
   three
   four
   five

4. Clothing
   shirt
   pants
   dress
   shoes
   hat

5. Pets
   cat
   dog
   bird
   fish
   rabbit

6. Furniture
   table
   chair
   sofa
   chest
   desk

7. Eating Objects
   cup
   plate
   bowl
   fork
   spoon

8. Transportation
   car
   truck
   bus
   plane
   boat

9. Food
   bread
   meat
   soup
   apple
   cereal

10. Drinks
    water
    milk
    juice
    soda
    malt

100 PICTURE NOUNS -- Continued

11. Numbers 6-10
six
seven
eight
nine
ten

12. Fruit
fruit
orange
grape
pear
banana

13. Plants
bush
flower
grass
plant
tree

14. Sky Things
sun
moon
star
cloud
rain

15. Earth Things
lake
rock
dirt
field
hill

16. Farm Animals
horse
cow
pig
chicken
duck

17. Workers
farmer
policeman
cook
doctor
nurse

18. Entertainment
television
radio
movie
ball game
band

19. Writing Tools
pen
pencil
crayon
chalk
computer

20. Reading Things
book
newspaper
magazine
sign
letter

PREFIXES

Prefix	Meaning	Example
anti-	against	antiwar, antinuclear, antisocial, antislavery
auto-	self	automobile, automatic, autograph, autobiography
bi-, bin-	two	bicycle, binocular, biceps, bifocal, biplane
cent-	hundred	centigrade, century, cent, centimeter
de-	opposite	deactivate, deform, degrade
dis-	opposite	disagree, dishonest, discontinue
im-	into	import, implant, immigrate
im-	not	imbalance, impossible, immature
inter-	among, between	interrupt, intermission, international, interpret, intervene
micro-	small, short	microphone, microscope, microbe, microfilm
mid-	middle	midnight, midsummer, midway, midyear

PREFIXES -- Continued

mis-	bad	misbehavior, misconduct, misfortune
non-	not	nonsense, nonconform, nondescript
over-	too much	overactive, overpriced, overdo
pre-	before	prefix, prejudice, precaution
re-	again	redo, rewrite, reappear, repaint, relive
semi-	half	semiannual, semicircle, semiconscious
sub-	under	submarine, subordinate, subterranean
super-	more than	superhuman, supernatural, superpower, superfine
tele-	distant	telephone, telescope, telegram, television
trans-	across	transatlantic, transcend, transfer, translate
tri-	three	triangle, tricycle, trillion, triplet
un-	not	unhappy, unable, unbeaten, uncertain, uncomfortable
under-	below	underneath, undercover, underground, underpass

GREEK ROOTS

Root	Meaning	Examples
aero	air	aerospace, aeronautics, aerosol, aeroplane (alternate spelling of airplane)
ast	star	astronaut, astronomy, disaster, asterisk
cycl	circle, ring	bicycle, cyclone, cycle, encyclopedia, cyclops
gram	letter, written	telegram, diagram, grammar, epigram, monogram
graph	write	telegraph, photograph, phonograph, autograph
meter	measure	thermometer, centimeter, diameter, barometer
phon	sound	phonograph, symphony, telephone, microphone, phonics
photo	light	photograph, photography, telephoto, photosynthesis
pop	people	population, popular, populace
scop	see	microscope, telescope, periscope, stethoscope
therm	heat	thermometer, thermal, thermostat, thermos

LATIN ROOTS

Root	Meaning	Examples
act	do	action, react, transact, actor, enact
ang	bend	angle, triangle, quadrangle, angular
aud	hear	auditorium, audience, audiovisual, audible, audition
credit	believe	credit, discredit, incredible, credulous
dict	speak	predict, contradict, dictate, verdict, diction
duc, duct	lead	conduct, aqueduct, duct, induct, educate
fac	make, do	factory, manufacture, benefactor, facsimile
loc	place	locate, dislocate, relocate, location, allocate
man	hand	manual, manufacture, manuscript, manipulate
migr	move	migrate, immigrant, emigrate, migratory
miss	send	missile, dismiss, missionary, mission, remiss

LATIN ROOTS -- Continued

mob	move	automobile, mobile, mobility, mobilize
mot	move	motion, motor, promote, demote, motile
ped	foot	pedal, pedestrian, biped, pedestal
pop	people	population, popular, pop, populace
port	carry	transport, import, portable, porter
rupt	break	erupt, interrupt, rupture, bankrupt, abrupt
sign	mark	signature, signal, significant, insignia
spec	see	inspect, suspect, respect, spectator, spectacle
tract	pull, drag	tractor, subtract, attraction, traction
urb	city	urban, suburb, suburban, urbane
vac	empty	vacant, vacation, vacuum, evacuate, vacate
vid	see	video, evidence, provide, providence

IMPORTANT SIGNS

DANGER	UP	MAIN FLOOR
KEEP OUT	LADIES	LOBBY
GAS	MEN	TICKETS
NO TRESPASSING	WOMEN	TAXI
WALK	HOT	TELEPHONE
POISON	COLD	MANAGER
NO SMOKING	DEPOSIT	OFFICE
EXIT	QUARTER	POST OFFICE
DOWN	FREE	FIRE ESCAPE

DEVELOP PHONICS SKILLS

You are doing a lot for your student. You have found his reading levels and have given him materials on which he can succeed in reading. You are encouraging him to practice reading, checking his comprehension, and helping him develop a basic reading vocabulary with the Instant Words.

You can help him in still another way. You can help him improve his reading by building phonics skills. The following pages will prepare you to use the Phonics Survey and the Phonics Charts effectively.

Place of Teaching Phonics

Teachers, like parents, often take violent positions "for" and "against" phonics. Interestingly enough, neither side can conclusively prove that the "phonics method" is better or worse than the "word method". Hence, most teachers hedge their bets and teach a little of each. We suggest that you do the same.

On the charts that follow, you will find most of the basic phonics rules arranged in a good order for teaching.

Some teachers who like phonics would start phonics on the first day and drill the children on letter sounds and example words. They would be sure to get through all these rules in the first grade.

A phonics moderate would start phonics lessons after the student had acquired a small sight word vocabulary (25 or 50 words). She would probably try to teach the material in the first few charts during the first year but would not be too upset with something less than perfect performance.

A phonics laggard would take three years to cover the material in these charts and then probably would have skipped or at best glossed over much of the material in Charts 6 and 7. Some basic reading series are in this category.

These "years" refer to children beginning at age six with average ability. Bright children, older children, and adults would of course go faster. And all can benefit from some review lessons on phonics.

Pre-phonics

All teachers would agree on the importance of first being sure that the student can make the speech sounds and that he can hear the difference between sounds. Children need to develop a skill called "phoneme awareness". This means knowing that all words are made up of relatively few sounds. The English language uses about 44 sounds of phonemes. For example, "cat" has 3 phonemes, /k/, /ă/, /t/. Phonics is learning the correlation between the spoken sound and its spelling or, in other words, the letter or letters that represent that sound. For example, the /k/ sound at the beginning of the word "cat" is spelled with a "c", the /ă/ sound with an "a", etc.

You can help develop this phoneme awareness by reading to your student poems and stories that have repetition of sounds (like Cat in the Hat), by pointing out the same sound in similar words (see Phonics Charts at the end of this chapter) and by other word patterns such as phonograms (see Phonogram Charts at the end of this chapter).

Good early phonics instruction occurs when students use invented spelling -- just trying to spell words by how they sound. Phonics instruction occurs when the student is helped to spell the word more accurately.

A little drill using the picture charts can also help a lot in hearing and making the sounds (see pages 81 to 89).

Whether or not to say the sounds in isolation is a problem you can solve for yourself. Personally, I do, but I am careful not to use a "schwa" sound ("uh") at the end of a consonant when it isn't needed. For example, I say, "nnn", not "nuh". Consonants that can be pronounced without a "schwa" are "T", "N", "R", "M", "S", "L", "P", "F", "V", "H", "K", "W", and the digraphs.

Some teachers say the sounds should only be taught as part of a word. Others say it is all right to pronounce a consonant with a vowel, but this group is divided (c-at or ca-t). The important point of phonics is that the student must learn that the letter or digraph (2 letters making 1 sound) stands for a sound. It is also helpful to learn common letter clusters like "-ump", to read and spell words like "bump, clump, dump", etc.

Diagnosing Phonics Skills

In phonics, as in everything else, a good teacher must know where a student is at the beginning, middle, and end of instruction.

For a simple test you can write a letter or digraph (two letters that make one sound, like "sh") on the board and ask the student what sound it makes. If you want to be a little trickier, ask him to sound out some nonsense syllables. Build into the nonsense word the thing you want to test. For example, if you want to know if he knows the digraphs on Chart 4, write "phiz" and if he says "fizz", you know that he knows some phonics.

The Phonics Survey that is on page 94 will help you to test skills systematically in the main phonics areas.

Methods of Teaching Phonics

Phonics Charts. The Phonics Charts at the end of this chapter give you a rather complete overview of what is usually taught in phonics in most schools. Turn through the pages so that you get the general idea. The Phonics Charts are arranged in a teaching order so we suggest that you teach the content of the first Chart, then the Second Chart, etc.

In phonics you are just trying to teach the letter sound connection. Don't worry if your student can't read all the words on the charts. The words and pictures are there just so that there will be some examples of the sounds that letter makes in a word.

Sometimes it takes 2 letters to make 1 sound; these 2 letter combinations are called "digraphs" and should be taught just as if the digraph was a single letter. For example, the digraph "sh" "blend" of "s" and "h", but a different sound (phoneme). "Blends" like the "bl" at the beginning of "black" are given in the last chart. Blends have 2 or 3 phonemes.

You will also note that some consonants (ex. "c", "g") and all vowels have several sounds. This is confusing for the student and requires a little practice. If he slowly masters the skills as they are presented in the order of these charts, it will cut down on the confusion.

Encourage your student to apply phonics when he is reading and can't pronounce a word. You can say, "Try sounding it out." Help him to do this. However, when trying to sound out unknown words you will quickly find that phonics rules don't always work. There are more rules than are presented on these charts and, beyond that, there are just many exceptions. Why should "sugar" have a "sh" sound at the beginning, or why does "of" have a "uv" sound? There just aren't enough rules to cover these things and that is why <u>many words have to be learned as sight words.</u> But do not despair; phonics does help in unlocking many words and phonics rules are also useful in some spelling lessons. Phonics rules also often help the student to sound out just part of the word. With this much information, plus context (how the word is used in a sentence), the student can get the word. For example, the first thing many reading teachers say when a student is stuck on a word is, "What sound does it begin with?"

Nobody ever said that it was easy to learn how to read. It takes time and practice spread out over years. Your student needs all the help he can get and phonics is just one way to help a little.

You can use the Phonics Charts to introduce some phonics skills like Easy Consonants or Short Vowels, then give a lot of practice in using them with practice words, games, and calling attention to these elements when reading.

Bingo. I have always liked to teach phonics in games. A game that works as well for phonics is "bingo". Make some bingo cards of the sounds on Chart 1 and call off the letter sounds, one at a time. (Don't use letter names - say "kh as in cat" not "cee".) You can also make different "pairs" games, teaching the children to use consonant sounds instead of Instant Words.

T	N	R
M	D	S
L	C	P

Bingo Card for Beginners

B	F	V	A	H
K	W	J	QU	X
Y	Z	TH	CH	WH
SH	PH	PR	ST	PL
TW	GL	SN	FR	SK

Bingo Card for more Advanced Students

Remember when making Bingo Cards that every player must have the same letters but in different arrangements. When calling letters, remember to use letter sounds, say "sss as is Sam" not the letter name such as "dee (d), es (s), are (r)", etc.

Spelling. Some teachers are quite successful teaching phonics along with spelling and writing. After an initial presentation of the first half of Charts 1 and 2, such a teacher might say, "Class, write sad on your papers." (Note that this gives every student a chance to participate.) After a minute, she has a pupil write the word correctly on the board. Then each student gets immediate knowledge of results to help his learning. Of course, the teacher chooses just phonetically regular words from among the sounds already introduced.

Some wild tutors, like me, might even call off nonsense words, such as "dat" and "nuv", just to test the pupils' abilities in phonics. Other teachers are more concerned that students know the meaning of each word. Whenever possible, these teachers have their pupils use each word in a sentence, and that is not a bad idea.

The Spelling Book (Laguna Beach Educational Books) mentioned earlier contains a lot of phonics instruction suggestions. And this shows that phonics can easily and effectively be taught in spelling lessons. As a teacher or tutor, you can take your choice and teach phonics as part of reading lessons, as part of spelling lessons, or both, which might be even better.

Phonograms. A phonogram is a group of letters containing a vowel and a consonant sound that needs another consonant sound to make a word. For example, the "-ail" phonogram can make words like "mail, tail, and sail" when different consonants are added.

At the end of this chapter you will find some phonograms and example words that you can use in teaching. There are many more phonograms, but these will get you started. You can find long lists of phonograms and many other types of words in The Reading Teacher's Book of Lists (Prentice Hall).

One way to use a phonogram is simply to write it on a piece of paper or chalkboard, then ask your student how many words he can make using that phonogram. You can help him a little.

Phonogram lists also make interesting spelling lessons. Give one or two phonogram families to your student, help him study them a little making sure that he can pronounce all the words, then give him a spelling test to see if he can spell them all. This is a great way to teach the sounds of different consonants and hence phonograms.

Phonograms also can be taught with many games and teaching devices. Word wheels, slide charts, and board games often use phonograms. These devices can be teacher made, student made or bought in school supply stores.

"Phonogram" is a reading teacher word. Some researchers call the same idea "onset and rhyme"; the "onset" is the initial consonant sound like "d-" and the "rhyme" is the ending vowel and consonant like "-og". Together they make "dog", which rhymes with "log, fog, bog", etc. Some linguists call the same idea "consonant substitution". Whatever you call it, try some of the examples on pages 90 to 93 for reading and spelling lessons.

You might want to start your phonics lessons by using the Phonics Survey on page 94. However, informally you can get a good idea of a student's phonics ability by asking a student to "sound out" unknown words. If sounding out a whole word is too difficult, you can just say "what sound does it begin with?" Or "Do you know some other words that have parts that look like parts of this word?"

Phonics Warning

The good part of phonics is that it helps the student to sound out unknown words and make rapid progress in reading. The bad part of phonics is that some teachers "beat it to death" with boring drills, and the student learns to hate reading and education in general.

Another caution about phonics is that if too much emphasis is placed on sounds and not enough on other skills in reading, such as comprehension, then children can become word-callers. They spit out the words orally but have no idea what they mean. Hence, balance your lessons – some word drill, some oral reading, some phonics, some silent reading, some comprehension drills, some spelling and writing lessons, and lots of easy reading in interesting books.

PHONICS CHARTS
EASY CONSONANTS

Phonics Chart 1

T top	**N** nut	**R** ring
to take tell not at it	not no new and in can	run red read from our for
M man	**D** dog	**S** saw
me my mother some from room	do day down good and said	some so see this us yes
L letter	**C** cat	**P** pencil
little like look will girl school	can come color because second music	put pretty page up jump stop
B book	**F** fish	**V** valentine
but be boy about remember tub	for from first if before off	very visit voice give leave have

PHONICS CHARTS -- Continued
EASY VOWELS

Phonics Chart 2

and at as add can bad man had	**A** apple	end egg every enjoy when get red men	**E** elephant
in is it inch with will little did	**I** Indian	on off ox October not box stop got	**O** ostrich

up us until under but much just funny	**U** umbrella

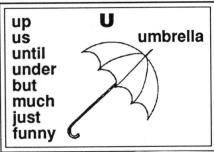

1. "E" at the end of a word The letter "E" is silent at the end of a word are some one like (These vowels are not long. See Chart 5 for final "E" rule.)	2. "Y" sounds like long "E" at the end of a word containing another vowel very many any pretty

PHONICS CHARTS -- Continued
DIFFICULT CONSONANTS
Phonics Chart 3

good **G** girl	have **H** hat
go	he
get	had
gas	home
again	her
dig	him
big	has
bag	hit

kind **K** king	we **W** window
keep	with
kill	will
key	was
like	away
make	between
work	twenty
book	sandwich

just **J** jar	quite **QU** queen
January	quart
jump	quick
joy	quack
object	square
enjoy	equal
major	squirrel
banjo	earthquake

six **X** box	yes **Y** yacht	zero **Z** zebra
ax	you	zoo
extra	year	zone
Texas	yellow	zipper
box	lawyer	lazy
ox	canyon	prize
tax		dozen
next	at the end of a	size
	short word, say	
	the long"I"sound	
	sky fry	
	my why	

PHONICS CHARTS -- Continued
CONSONANT DIGRAPHS AND SECOND SOUNDS
Phonics Chart 4

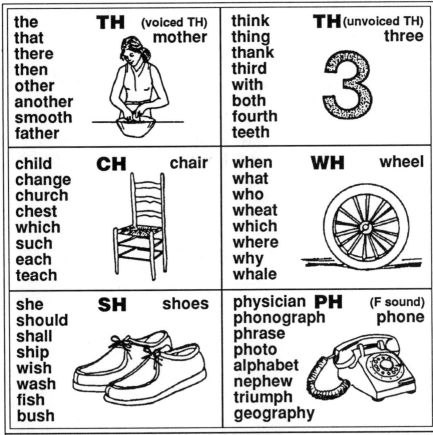

TH (voiced TH) mother	**TH** (unvoiced TH) three
the that there then other another smooth father	think thing thank third with both fourth teeth

CH chair	**WH** wheel
child change church chest which such each teach	when what who wheat which where why whale

SH shoes	**PH** (F sound) phone
she should shall ship wish wash fish bush	physician phonograph phrase photo alphabet nephew triumph geography

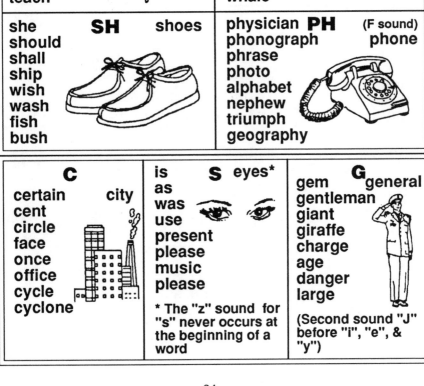

C city	**S** eyes*	**G** general
certain cent circle face once office cycle cyclone	is as was use present please music please * The "z" sound for "s" never occurs at the beginning of a word	gem gentleman giant giraffe charge age danger large (Second sound "J" before "i", "e", & "y")

PHONICS CHARTS -- Continued
LONG VOWELS
Phonics Chart 5

FINAL "E" RULE: An E at the end of a word frequently makes the vowel long and the "E" is silent.

A-E		I-E	
make	ate	white	time
take	age	while	fire
came	ace	five	nine
made	able	write	mile
name	ape	ride	like
O-E		**U-E**	
home	alone	use	
those	nose	produce	
close	bone	lube	
hope	pole	pure	
note	rose	tube	

Note: long "E" is omitted because of its infrequency.

PHONICS CHARTS -- Continued
LONG VOWELS

Phonics Chart 5 - continued

OPEN SYLLABLE RULE: When a syllable ends in a vowel, that vowel frequently has the long sound.

A	E	I	O	U
April	we	I	so	duty
paper	be	idea	go	pupil
lady	he	pilot	no	music
baby	me	tiny	open	student
radio	even	lion	hello	January

DOUBLE VOWEL RULE: When two vowels are together, frequently the first vowel is long and the second one is silent. These are also known as vowel digraphs. There are only six common ones.

EA	EE	AI	AY	OA	OW
eat	see	fail	stay	coat	own
year	three	remain	day	soap	know
please	seem	train	gray	road	show
easy	sleep	aid	clay	oak	yellow
sea	tree	chain	crayon	loan	bowl

PHONICS CHARTS -- Continued
"SCHWA" AND VOWEL PLUS "R"
Phonics Chart 6

SCHWA: The unaccented vowel in a word frequently has the sound of A in "ago".

a A	a E	a O
about	happen	official
again	problem	oppose
away	bulletin	money
several	hundred	canyon
China	united	

"ER", "IR", AND "UR" frequently all make the same sound.

ER	IR	UR
her	first	turn
were	dirt	hurt
other	third	fur
after	sir	hurry
camera	circus	Thursday

"AR" has two sounds:
"AR" as in far; "AR" as in vary   "OR" has a unique
           ("air" sound)   "O" sound

AR		OR
/ar/	/ar/	
star	library	for
are	vary	or
far	Mary	before
start	care	more
hard	January	horn
car	share	

PHONICS CHARTS -- Continued
DIPHTHONGS AND OTHER VOWEL SOUNDS

Phonics Chart 7

Broad "O" sound is made by "O", "AL", "AW", and "AU".

O	AL	AW	AU
on	all	draw	because
long	salt	law	author
upon	also	awful	August
off	talk	lawn	haul
song	call	straw	daughter

Diphthongs make sliding sound from one vowel sound to another.

OI	OY	OU	OW
OI and OY make the same sound		OU and OW make the same sound	
point	annoy	out	how
voice	enjoy	about	down
noise	toy	our	brown
oil	royal	round	now
boil	oyster	loud	flower

Double "O" and Short "EA"

OO		EA	Second sound of EA
Double O			
long sound	short sound	Short EA sound	
soon	good	dead	
school	foot	ahead	
too	look	heavy	
room	took	ready	
zoo	cook	feather	

Silent letters

KN	K before N is silent	GH	GH is usually silent
knife		eight	
knee		high	
know		might	
knot		light	
knight		right	
knit		caught	

88

PHONICS CHARTS -- Continued
CONSONANT BLENDS

Phonics Chart 8

R Family

PR - pretty	prince	prize	April
TR - truck	trick	true	extra
GR - grapes	green	grand	hungry
BR - bread	brick	bring	zebra
CR - crab	cry	crow	across
DR - drum	drug	dress	hundred
FR - frog	free	from	afraid

S Family

ST - stamp	stop	stone	best
SP - spoon	sport	spring	crisp
SC - scout	scrub	screw	scoop
SK - skate	sky	skin	mask
SW - swing	swim	sweep	swell
SM - smile	smell	smoke	smart
SN - snow	snake	snap	snooze

L Family

PL - plate	play	please	supply
CL - clock	class	cloud	include
BL - black	blue	blood	tumbler
FL - flag	flower	fly	snowflake
SL - slow	sleep	sled	asleep
GL - glass	glad	glory	angle

Orphan

TW - twins	twelve	twice	between

PHONOGRAMS

-ack (ă)	-ad (ă)	-ail (ā)	-ain (ā)
back	bad	bail	gain
hack	dad	fail	lain
Jack	fad	Gail	main
lack	had	hail	pain
Mack	lad	jail	rain
pack	mad	mail	vain
quack	pad	nail	brain
rack	sad	pail	chain
sack	tad	quail	drain
tack	Brad	rail	grain
black	Chad	sail	plain
clack	clad	tail	slain
crack	glad	wail	Spain
knack	shad	frail	sprain
shack		snail	stain
smack		trail	strain
snack			train

-ake (ā)	-an (ă)	-ap (ă)	-are (ă)
bake	ban	cap	bare
cake	can	gap	care
fake	Dan	lap	dare
Jake	fan	map	fare
lake	man	nap	mare
make	pan	rap	rare
quake	ran	sap	blare
rake	tan	tap	flare
sake	van	chap	glare
take	bran	clap	scare
wake	clan	flap	share
brake	flan	scrap	snare
drake	plan	slap	spare
flake	scan	snap	square
shake	span	strap	stare
snake	than	trap	

PHONOGRAMS -- Continued

-ash (ă)	-at (ă)	-ed (ĕ)	-eed (ē)
bash	bat	bed	deed
cash	cat	fed	feed
dash	fat	led	heed
gash	gnat	Ned	need
hash	hat	red	reed
lash	mat	Ted	seed
mash	pat	wed	weed
rash	rat	bled	bleed
sash	sat	bred	breed
brash	tat	fled	creed
clash	vat	Fred	freed
crash	brat	shed	greed
flash	chat	shred	speed
slash	drat	sled	steed
smash	flat	sped	treed
stash	scat		
thrash	slat		
trash	spat		

-ell (ĕ)	-ew (ü)	-ick (ĭ)	-ight (ī)
bell	dew	Dick	fight
cell	few	kick	knight
dell	hew	lick	light
fell	Jew	Nick	might
hell	knew	pick	night
jell	pew	quick	right
Nell	blew	Rick	sight
sell	brew	sick	tight
tell	chew	tick	blight
well	crew	wick	bright
yell	drew	brick	flight
dwell	flew	chick	fright
quell	screw	click	plight
shell	skew	flick	slight
smell	slew	slick	

PHONOGRAMS -- Continued

-in (ĭ)	-ine (ī)	-ing (ĭ)	-ink (ĭ)
bin	dine	bing	kink
din	fine	ding	link
fin	line	king	mink
gin	mine	ping	pink
kin	nine	ring	rink
pin	pine	sing	sink
sin	tine	wing	wink
tin	vine	zing	blink
win	wine	bring	brink
chin	brine	cling	chink
grin	shine	fling	clink
shin	shrine	sling	drink
skin	spine	spring	shrink
spin	swine	sting	stink
thin	whine	string	think
twin		swing	

-it (ĭ)	-ob (ŏ)	-ock (ŏ)	-od (ŏ)
bit	Bob	dock	cod
fit	cob	hock	God
hit	fob	knock	mod
kit	gob	lock	nod
knit	job	mock	pod
lit	knob	rock	rod
pit	lob	sock	sod
quit	mob	tock	Tod
sit	rob	block	clod
wit	sob	clock	plod
flit	blob	crock	prod
grit	slob	flock	shod
skit	snob	frock	trod
slit		shock	
spit		smock	
split		stock	

PHONOGRAMS -- Continued

-op (ŏ)	-ore (ô)	-ot (ŏ)	-ub (ŭ)
bop	bore	cot	cub
cop	core	got	dub
hop	fore	hot	hub
mop	gore	jot	nub
pop	more	knot	pub
sop	pore	lot	rub
top	sore	not	sub
chop	tore	pot	tub
crop	wore	rot	club
drop	shore	tot	flub
flop	score	blot	grub
plop	spore	clot	scrub
prop	store	plot	shrub
shop	swore	shot	snub
slop		slot	stub
stop		spot	

-uck (ŭ)	-ug (ŭ)	-um (ŭ)	-ump (ŭ)
buck	bug	bum	bump
duck	dug	gum	dump
huck	hug	hum	hump
luck	jug	mum	jump
muck	lug	rum	lump
puck	mug	sum	pump
suck	pug	yum	rump
tuck	rug	chum	sump
Chuck	tug	drum	chump
cluck	chug	glum	clump
pluck	drug	plum	frump
shuck	plug	scum	grump
stuck	shrug	slum	plump
struck	slug	strum	slump
truck	smug	swum	stump

For additional phonograms and phonic example words, see *The Reading Teacher's Book of Lists* cited on the inside of the back cover.

PHONICS SURVEY DIRECTIONS

Phonics is an important and useful skill associated with reading. Poor ability in phonics does not always mean poor reading ability, but if reading ability is poor, it can often be aided by having part of the instruction include phonics lessons.

How to Test. Using the test on the next page, ask the student to read the nonsense words aloud. Tell him that these are not real words. If he makes an error, allow him a second chance (but not a third).

How to Score. Using a copy of the record sheet below, mark each letter read incorrectly. At the right-hand margin, note if the student was "Perfect", "Knew Some", or "Knew None" for each of the following skills: Consonants, Short Vowels, Long Vowels, Difficult Vowels. This information will be very useful in selection materials for phonics instruction.

PHONICS SURVEY

This survey gives a general idea of the amount of phonics skills known by the student.

Name _____

Examiner_____ Date_____

Student reads nonsense words using phonics rules. Teacher checks box to right of line according to amount known.	Perfect	Knew Some	Knew None

Section 1-Easy Consonants and Short Vowels
　　　　　Charts 1 & 2

TIF	**NEL**	**ROM**	☐	☐	☐
DUP	**CAV**	**SEB**	☐	☐	☐

Section 2-Harder Consonants and Long Vowels
　　　　　Charts 3 & 5

KO	**HOAB**	**WAJE**	**KE**	**YATE** ☐	☐	☐
ZEEX	**QUIDE**	**YAIG**	**ZAY**	**SUDE** ☐	☐	☐

Section 3-Consonant Digraphs and Difficult
　　　　　Vowels
　　　　　Charts 4, 6, & 7

WHAW	**THOIM**	**PHER**	**KOYCH**	☐	☐	☐
OUSH	**CHAU**	**EANG**	**HOON**	☐	☐	☐

This survey may be repeated at a later date after more phonics instruction, or the teacher can make up nonsense words for testing or instruction.

WRITING, SPEAKING, LISTENING

Some years ago in Africa I saw what I shall always think of as the minimum school. It consisted of a tree, a chair, and a small box of books. There was no furniture for the students; they sat on the bare ground. This school had no walls, no windows, no electricity, no chalkboard, no basal readers, practically no library, and no pencils or paper. I often think of it when I hear teachers complain about lack of books or supplies.

Yet this minimum school had many advantages. The setting was beautiful: birds sang and butterflies floated through the classroom. The air was fresh and the lighting excellent. No bells rang to end lessons and no principal provided rules. The teacher had to be creative, and he was. He was conducting a very good elementary reading lesson. "How?", you might ask, when he had nothing. Well he didn't quite have nothing. Most importantly he had some knowledge of teaching techniques and secondly he had a long, straight stick.

He had the students take the stick and smooth a section of bare ground. Then, with a twig, plucked from a nearby bush, he had the students draw lines in the dirt, using the stick as a ruler. And on those lines students wrote stories in small groups: one student writing, others helping with spelling and story suggestions, then all students reading the story when it was written. The students were divided into groups and one group read the other group's stories and talked about them. The teacher helped the students get started, aided in correcting spelling and grammar and, of course, provided the atmosphere for creative writing and the discipline that got the story written and read. He also later had most of the students write some of the words used in the story with their own twigs in the smoothed dirt.

The children were very proud to show me their stories and I have been grateful for the rest of my life for the experience. Never again will I take too seriously a teacher's complaints that she can't teach reading well because she doesn't have enough books, or the proper books, or enough supplies, or a new chalkboard, or a classroom that isn't in good shape.

Incidentally, the children had on minimal clothing. Most had just a string tied around their middle. After all, it wouldn't be proper to come to school with nothing on, would it?

Language Experience Approach

Now the teaching method the teacher was using is well known in the United States and is called various names, such as the Language Experience Approach, or the Whole Language method, because it integrates reading, writing, speaking and listening. United States teachers usually have chalkboards, paper charts with felt tip pens, pencil and paper, or more recently, small computers with word processing programs, but the basic ideas are the same as the African teacher with his twigs and dirt.

1. Motivate the student (or a group) to write a story.
2. Have most students read the story.
3. Discuss it, extend it, correct it.

Sounds simple, doesn't it. Why then doesn't everybody use it all the time? There are a lot of reasons. Some teachers find it hard to get students to be creative writers all the time. Using books extends the student's reading and thinking experiences. Some students do better with a more structured approach, which might include basic sight vocabularies, phonics and varieties of comprehension questions. But a lot of teachers use story writing and some Whole Language teaching for part of their reading lessons. And you can too.

Story Starters

To get a story out of a student or a group, the teacher often has to help the writing get started. Some teachers use a recent group experience like rain on the playground, a trip to the zoo, a job change.

Another technique for getting stories started is to use a Story Starter, which is a phrase or a suggested title like:

My favorite place to be . . .
Don't you hate it when . . .
In the year 2020 . . .

There are a lot more Story Starters at the end of this Chapter and you can probably think up some of your own. Also, as suggested earlier, some of the items on the Interest Inventory in Step 2 can be used as Story Starters.

Experience Charts

One version of story writing that is used more with beginning readers, who do not have much writing ability, is for the teacher to do the writing on a large piece of paper or a chalkboard as the students dictate a story. This can be done with a single student or a small group.

The basic idea is that the students tell a short story while the teacher or tutor writes it down. Then the students read the story to the teacher.

To get started, the student can suggest a title or the teacher can provide a bit of motivation by using a Story Starter.

After a title is written down the teacher can help the dictation by saying something like, "Now what do you want to say about...?"

The teacher must be careful to write in short, easy sentences. It is all right for the teacher to modify the student's dictation a bit by writing correct grammar and using easy vocabulary. Especially in the beginning, the story should be short. Remember the student or students are going to have to read back the whole story and learn to read all the new words used.

The story need not be completed in one lesson. The teacher might just write a sentence or two, then add to the story the next day. Of course, each day the previous parts of the story are reviewed with the student trying to read it, with as little help from the teacher as necessary.

The teacher should take words out of the story and see if the student can read them. This prevents students from just memorizing the whole story and not really knowing how to read the individual words. It is not bad for the student to become so familiar with a story that it is almost memorized, but it is a good reading lesson to make sure that the student also knows how to read each of the words in the story. Take a look again at Step 4 for other techniques for teaching individual words.

You should also do some kind of comprehension check on the story just so the student gets the idea that, for all reading, comprehension is essential. Step 3 has a lot of suggestions on varying the type of questions and other comprehension teaching techniques.

Writing the student's stories on a sheet of paper or on a large paper chart has one advantage over a chalkboard: they can be saved and read later, at the end of a week, or month, or even year. Sometimes students like to look back at their earlier lessons to see how far they have come in reading more advanced material.

But with Experience Charts, as with any other type of lesson, keep it easy enough to be successful. Frustrate your student too often and you won't have any student -- you might have a body, but the mind will be elsewhere.

Student-written Stories

As students develop more skills in writing, they can write their own stories. They can do this using any paper and pencil. Schools often use lined paper with wider lines for young children, but this is not necesssary. Most schools now urge student writers to use "invented spelling" on their first draft. This means that the student should write the story to get the ideas down and worry about correct spelling later. The same is true for grammar. It can be corrected on a later draft.

Not every story has to be polished. Sometimes the student can just write a short, interesting story and read it to the teacher or to the class. Other times the student should polish a story more by having the teacher or superior student look it over and suggest better spelling or better grammar.

Incidentally, writing is developmental just like reading and speaking. In speaking, for example, the child first babbles, then has one word sentences, then simple vocabulary and slightly longer sentences. At first, speech sounds are not complete and some words come out mispronounced in "baby talk". The same things happen in writing, but at an older age. Writing development goes from scribbling, to crude letters, to invented spelling, to short stories with simple vocabulary and later to more mature writing. So don't get excited if beginning writers are not perfect writers. Help them to progress a little bit at a time. Give them a lot of encouragement at any stage and don't yell loudly about mistakes. Not every story needs to be a show piece. Get the ideas down. Practice makes for fluency.

Older students and adults might enjoy writing whole little books composed of a collection of stories. Some teachers type up these student stories and bind them along with student art for illustrations. If you have several students, they can read each other's stories or books.

Handwriting

At the end of this chapter are several Handwriting Charts that can be used to teach handwriting. For beginners, it is not too hard. Just have them practice on a few letters at a time using the Manuscript Alphabet. Then they can combine the letters into words. All beginners need occasional correction and sometimes more practice on certain letters that they form poorly when writing stories.

There are several popular systems of forming letters. The one at the end of this chapter is just one that is widely used. Most schools will give anyone a copy of the handwriting chart they are using.

In most public schools, somewhere near the end of second grade or the beginning of third grade, the students are taught the Cursive Alphabet, which most adults use for everyday writing. Though this is the popular custom, it is not necessary to learn Cursive Handwriting. In Europe, many people spend all their lives writing with essentially Manuscript handwriting. Some educators argue that all children should only be taught Manuscript handwriting because it is more legible and just as fast. Incidentally, Manuscript handwriting is legal for signatures on checks and other documents.

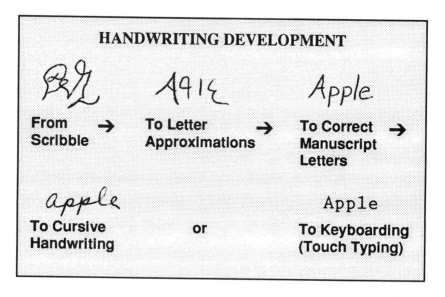

HANDWRITING DEVELOPMENT

From Scribble → To Letter Approximations → To Correct Manuscript Letters →

To Cursive Handwriting   or   To Keyboarding (Touch Typing)

One of the arguments for teaching just Manuscript is that it helps students to see words formed in a style that is closer to the kind of print seen in books and newspapers. Another argument for Manuscript is that when the student reaches third grade or fourth grade ability, he should be taught to type using the regular 10-finger ("touch") system. This is not hard to do. It only takes about 4 weeks of lessons. If you want to try it, get any old typewriter or a home computer with a word processing program and follow the lessons in my little book, *"Computer Keyboarding For Beginners"* (Laguna Beach Educational Books). It works for adults, too. High school remedial students often find learning to type makes their reading and writing lessons more "adult".

An argument in favor of teaching typing, or "keyboarding", is that in the near future many jobs will require keyboarding skills. Also, in some high schools and colleges, papers must be typed and often computers are used for homework. We have taught many children between fourth grade and junior high age and found that it just takes a little discipline and practice to learn a skill that will be of great value for a lifetime.

Maybe someday all schools will skip Cursive handwriting and just go from Manuscript straight to keyboarding.

For spelling lesson suggestions, see page 54.

Expository Writing

We have been talking about writing as though "stories" are the only things students write or read. This is not so. Expository writing means non-story writing. Expository writing includes such things as autobiographies, news stories, text books, directions, form filling, and advertisements. Your student will need to know how to do this type of writing also, as well as having some practice with this type of reading.

Adult literacy students especially appreciate the functional need for expository writing and reading. In many adult classes, the writing gets very practical. Students fill out job applications, post office forms, and work reports.

Learning to write helps learning to read and learning to read helps learning to write. So, practice both.

Speaking

Speaking is oral composition of words just as writing is written composition of words. It will help your student's writing if he or she is given plenty of opportunities to talk. Sometimes, just let your student tell a story or describe something. Encourage the development of ideas and use of new words. Do not, for heaven's sake, make fun or joke about wrong word use -- sometimes permit it and sometimes gently suggest a more correct word use. It is through experimenting and trying out that we all learned to talk and hopefully are still learning to talk because, like reading and writing, speaking is a life-long developmental process. So, encourage use of new or partially known words. Encourage wild ideas and conventional ideas. Take some time to just listen to your student. Some of the worst teachers are those who talk all the time.

Incidentally, don't get too excited about speech errors or "baby talk", especially with young children or ESL students. It is normal for children to not be able to make all the English speech sounds (phonemes) until about age 6. It is also normal for children coming from houses where another language is spoken to not be able to make all the English speech sounds. For example, the Spanish language has no /j/ sound that we hear at the beginning of "general". Note that the Spanish boy's name, "Juan", sounds like it begins with a "w" sound. Every language in the world has a slightly different set of speech sounds (phonemes) -- so don't expect perfect enunciation for young children or ESL students, but you can gently suggest correction. Since all speech sounds are based on mechanical mouth positions and breath, you can often help correct speech errors by simply letting the student see you form the letters and by looking in a mirror letting him see himself making the sound. The Phonics Charts can give you some practice words for most speech sounds.

If your student hasn't shown definite progress after a year, you might consult the speech therapist in your local public school (even if your student goes to a private school). But the first rule is "don't get excited" on discovering any speech problem and don't rush off to all sorts of specialists and make a big deal out of it. Most students grow out of speech problems, especially if you help them a little. In the meantime, do not, under any circumstances, embarrass them.

Listening

We all learn to talk by listening. If our mothers, fathers, and playmates all spoke Chinese, we would all speak Chinese. But beyond this basic fact, listening to stories read to us helps us to talk better, read better, and write better. So many educators recommend that you READ TO STUDENTS EVERY DAY.

Many good parents read daily to their pre-schoolers and that is an excellent idea but unfortunately they stop when the child gets into elementary school. When I was a 6th grade teacher, I read several whole books to my class, a little bit each day, and they loved it. You can't be too old to listen. There are several very successful companies selling "books on tape". They sell these not to blind or illiterate or young children, but to business executives to listen to in their cars while commuting or in their bathrooms while shaving. In many public libraries you can check out audio tapes of both children's stories and adult books. But for children, there is nothing like having a parent or a teacher read to them.

While books and stories are usually thought of for listening experiences, you can also read all sorts of material, like news articles or directions to be followed.

Listening is good for students because:

1. It improves vocabulary. They learn word use and they hear words that might not be in everyday speech.
2. It improves grammar because they hear correct usage and variety in sentence construction.
3. It expands their thinking. They are temporarily transported to the world of tigers or space ships, or different kinds of families. They see that language can be fun.
4. Students can listen to harder stories than they can read for themselves so there is an expanded choice of reading material. But one long-term goal of reading instruction is that they be able to read for themselves anything that they can understand by listening.

So, if you don't do anything else suggested in this book, if you don't give any tests, don't teach any phonics or Instant Words, don't ask any comprehension questions, or don't require any written stories, the least you can do is read to your student(s).

Learn to read numbers

Students learning to read often do not know how to read numbers, particularly large numbers. Start out teaching some low numbers like "22", "96", "45", and work your way up to "123", "541", or "8,700".

STORY STARTERS LIST

Use these as suggested story titles or opening phrases for the first sentence. Also, see the Interest Inventories on pages 27 and 28 for Story Starter suggestions.

I often remember . . .
If I were a cloud . . .
My family . . .
I never . . .
The best vacation . . .
A barking dog means . . .
What would happen if . . .
Accidents are caused by . . .
Once I got lost . . .
People think that I . . .
The biggest problem in the world is . . .
The latest fashion . . .
I get mad when . . .
The farthest away from home I've been . . .
I dream about . . .
The phone rang at 3 A.M. . . .
Ants think about . . .
I want to know more about . . .
Just for fun we could . . .
The most beautiful thing I ever saw . . .
Rain always . . .

HANDWRITING CHARTS

Zaner-Bloser Manuscript Alphabet

Zaner-Bloser Cursive Alphabet

Zaner-Bloser   6116

Used with permission from *Handwriting: Basic Skills and Application.* Copyright© 1984 Zaner-Bloser, Inc., Columbus, Ohio

107

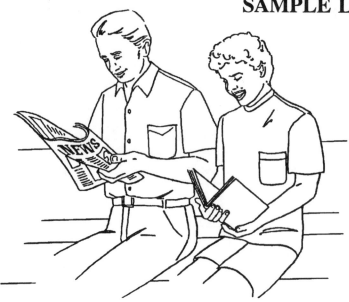

CONCLUSION AND SAMPLE LESSONS

A book on reading should be long enough to cover the subject and short enough to be interesting. I hope that this one has been long enough for you, but if not, any college library and most public libraries have plenty of books on reading that are longer.

These six steps should give you enough information to help you start teaching reading. They also give some additional suggestions for improvement if you already have some experience teaching reading. Actually, the six steps are the basic techniques used by many experienced classroom and remedial reading teachers.

Some Best Ideas

I recently had the pleasant experience of editing a book entitled The 10 Best Ideas For Reading Teachers, in which forty-four nationally recognized reading experts gave some of their best ideas about teaching reading. Practically every idea mentioned in the preceding chapters was mentioned by at least several of those reading specialists. But you might be interested in a few additional ideas of theirs that you can use:

- Use reading materials from other school subjects like science or social studies.

- Include drama (plays) for oral reading, speaking and listening experiences.

- Write every day. For example, keep a journal or diary.

- Write summaries of what you read. Write a letter to a friend.

- Parents and teachers should set a good example by reading themselves, often. Some suggest a regular quiet time for reading.

- Use graphic organizers, like making a time line for history or directions, a flow chart of a story, or cluster of characteristics associated with a vocabulary word.

- Use a computer with a word processor or a typewriter for story writing (if you do, please teach your student to keyboard-type with the 10 finger method).

- Join a book club.

- Try reading captioned television.

- Reread the same story over and over again, not just until oral errors disappear, but until reasonable speed and fluency do appear.

- Occasionally repeat assessment tasks like the Oral Paragraphs, Phonics Survey, or the Silent Reading Test.

- If you spot reading problems, tackle them early - don't wait.

- Read for pleasure; read about real things; read logos (like Coca Cola, Kleenex, etc.).

- Expand vocabulary any way you can: by wide reading, speaking, and picking words out of reading selections and discussing them.

- Emphasize comprehension. Form questions before, during and after reading. Ask the student to recall, summarize and compare.

- Develop background knowledge about a reading selection; talk about the setting, the characters, similar circumstances or similar subject matter.

- Kids are all different. They develop at different rates, have different interests, and have different abilities.

- Get a joke book. Read one a day.

- Learning to read is a complex, life-long process. You are not going to develop a mature reader in one month or even one year, but you can certainly move your student ahead a notch in that length of time and that, after all, is all any teacher can do.

Sample Lessons

Well, you have been exposed to a lot of ideas on how to teach reading, but exactly how do you start? What does a lesson consist of? Here are a few sample lessons for two boys of different reading ability:

1. Billy is a very beginning reader. He has almost no reading ability.

and

2. Juan who has some reading ability. He actually reads at about the 3rd or 4th grade ability level.

Sample Lessons

Billy -- reads practically nothing

1. Give Oral Reading Test (page 118). He scores Frustration Level on 1-A.

2. He helps you write an Experience Chart (page 99).

    Limit Chart story to a title and two short sentences.
    Limit words used -- mostly from first ten Instant Words (page 58) and first ten Picture nouns (page 66).

3. Billy rereads the Chart Story several times for fluency.

4. Billy helps you make a simple Bingo Game (page 52).

5. He makes two Bingo Cards using good handwriting (page 107), and you make two cards. Each card has nine words (three columns, three rows) from Chart Story Words.

6. You play Bingo.

7. You read part of a book to him (see Booklist page 29).

8. You ask him some questions based on book (see Comprehension Questions pages 35 to 37).

9. Praise Billy for good work.

Sample Lessons

Bill's second lesson

1. Billy rereads yesterday's Experience Chart. You help him with words he has forgotten.

2. Add two new short sentences to the Chart story. Billy suggests sentences; you write. Try to use a few more first ten words from Instant Words and Picture Nouns.

3. Billy rereads the story several times to improve fluency.

4. You take one of the words and show him it can be a phonogram. For example, "it" can become "hit" and "sit".

5. Have Billy write a "b" and an "m" before "it".

6. Play Bingo with yesterday's cards.

7. Give Billy a five-word spelling test using Chart story and phonogram words.

8. Correct paper and have Billy study words missed.

9. Read more of the story book.

10. Ask questions on the story.

11. Praise Billy for good work.

Sample Lessons

Billy's future lessons include:

1. More of the similar components of Lessons 1 and 2.

2. Soon introduce books for Billy to read with your help (see reading material pages 29 and 30).

3. Soon Billy should try writing his own short story with your help.

4. You or Billy can make a set of flash cards for words learned and new Instant Words (page 58).

5. After every few lessons you should reread sections of this book so that your lessons have plenty of variety.

Sample Lessons

Juan -- reads something

1. Give Oral Reading Test (page 118). He scores Instruction Level 3-B.

2. Have Juan fill out part of an Interest Inventory (page 27). You help him. If it goes too slowly, take two or three lessons to complete it.

3. Give Juan the Instant Word Oral Reading Test (page 64).

4. Play the Pairs game with Juan (page 52).

5. Read to Juan part of a book (see Booklist on page 29).

6. Use some discussion questions (pages 35 to 37) on the story.

7. Praise Juan for being so cooperative.

Sample Lessons

Juan's second lesson

1. Bring a book based on Oral Test (3rd grade difficulty) and based on his interest inventory. Discuss the book.

2. Help him read a small section of the book orally.

3. Have him reread the book silently.

4. Have him answer two questions orally and two questions by writing (see questions pages 35 to 37).

5. Do all or part of Brief Phonics Survey (page 94).

6. Use a Phonics Chart with example words on an error discovered in Phonics Survey.

7. Read to Juan from yesterday's story book.

8. Praise Juan for making progress.

Sample Lessons

Juan's future lessons include

1.   Continuation and extension of elements in Lessons 1 and 2. These are:
        Practice reading
        Improve vocabulary
        Learn phonics
        Teach Comprehension

2.   Have Juan write his own stories, letters, posters, etc.

3.   Spelling lessons based on words he needed while writing and the Instant Word List. See spelling suggestions on page 54.

4.   Vocabulary building based on words in stories and roots (pages 70-72 and Step 4).

5.   Use variety in Juan's reading instruction books and Juan's listening books (see Step 3).

6.   Lots of praise.

The Last Word

Oh, I forgot to tell you that Billy, who reads almost nothing, is a lot older than Juan. But you didn't ask. And that's right. Don't give reading lessons by age or size or language background. Start your lessons where the student is. And move your student ahead in little steps so that your student is continually being successful, because his success is your success too.

Rather than try to summarize this book, I might suggest that you reread the "one-paragraph" description of how to teach reading that starts on page 7 and also reread the Overview Section.

For teachers and students alike, there is no substitute for practice. Hence, you should practice teaching reading and practice improving your technique. After you practice teaching reading, reread applicable portions of this book. You may find them a good bit more interesting after you are face-to-face with a real live problem.

Last, but not least, I'd like to say that the ability to teach reading is a wonderful skill. When you teach a child or an illiterate adult how to read, you have given him or her a priceless gift that will keep on giving for a lifetime.

LONGER TESTS

Directions for the Oral Reading Test

Basically, the student reads aloud from one copy of the test while the examiner marks another copy.

The student copy of the Oral Reading Test is located next on pages 121 through 123 . The examiner asks the student to begin reading from the student's copy.

The examiner can make a copy of the Examiner's xerox copy of the Oral Reading Test Record Sheet (pages 125 through 127) or just use the copy in this book for scoring.

Scoring. Count one mistake for each word the student is unable to pronounce. If he immediately corrects himself, this is not counted as a mistake. If a student omits a word, ask him to read the line again more carefully.

Underline each word the student can't pronounce or needs help in pronouncing. When he has finished reading a paragraph, count the mistakes and check the appropriate line to the right of each paragraph.

For example, if a student begins with Paragraph 1-B and reads it without a mistake, or with 1 or 2 mistakes, he can read at this level independently.   Check "Independent" to the right of the paragraph.

The student should then read Paragraph 2-A. If he receives a score of 0-2 mistakes, then he can handle material at this level independently, too. Check "Independent".

He next reads Paragraph 2-B. If he makes 3-4 mistakes, you have found his Instructional Reading Level. Check "Instructional" to the right of that paragraph. This is the level at which reading instruction will be most effective for that student.

Notice that the number of mistakes for each reading level is shown on the test to the right of the paragraph. The number of mistakes varies. In Paragraphs 1-A through 2-B, 3 to 4 mistakes yield a student's Instructional Reading Level. However, 2 to 3 mistakes give the Instructional Reading Level in Paragraphs 3-A and 3-B, and only 2 mistakes do so in Paragraphs 4 through 7.

After finding the student's Instruction Reading Level, continue the test until you find his Frustration Reading Level. In Paragraphs 3-A and 3-B, 4 or more mistakes in a single paragraph would yield his Frustration Reading Level. In Paragraphs 4 through 7, 3 or more mistakes would yield his Frustration Reading Level. Stop testing when you get to his Frustration Level.

Record the results of the test in the spaces provided on the first page of the test. Fill in the highest grade level of material that the student can handle independently. Then record the grade level of material that should be used with him for instruction.

DO NOT use this test for instruction. If a student misses a word, tell him to "go on". Do not supply any hints or tell him the word. If this policy is followed, the same test can be used later to determine progress. When retesting a student, use different color pencils to underline mistakes. Spaces have been provided for recording results of retests.

Keep the record sheet for easy reference and for retesting.

Speed. The paragraphs are not timed, but excessive rapidity or slowness may be noted to the right of the paragraph as an important characteristic of the student's reading ability. Slow reading means more practice is needed at that level so the student can gain fluency.

Grade Levels of the Paragraphs. There are two paragraphs per grade level for grades 1 through 3. The first paragraph is marked 1-A. This means "easy first grade". The next is marked 1-B. This means "hard first grade".

There is only one paragraph for each level beyond third.

The last paragraph is marked grade 7, but actually it is indicative of popular adult and non-academic or non-technical secondary reading levels. If a student can read it perfectly, he can do most junior and senior high school readings satisfactorily. For more accurate determination of reading ability for students reading at junior and senior high school levels, a standardized silent reading test is recommended.

Comprehension. The Oral Reading Test does not measure comprehension. For most elementary reading levels, it is fairly safe to assume that comprehension roughly equals oral reading ability, but certainly comprehension is a skill well worth measuring.

The Reading Comprehension Tests located on pages 128 through 139 , and discussed in Step 3, will help you assess your students' silent reading comprehension.

ORAL READING TEST - STUDENT COPY
Have student read from this copy.

No. 1-A

Look at the dog.
It is big.
It can run.
Run dog, run away.

No. 1-B

We saw the sun.
It made us warm.
Now it was time to go home.
It was a long way to walk.

No. 2-A

The door of the house opened and a man came out.
He had a broom in his hand. He said to the boy
sitting there, "Go away." The boy got up and left.

No. 2-B

The family ate their breakfast. Then they gave the
pig his breakfast. It was fun to watch him eat. He
seemed to like it. He is eating all of it.

ORAL READING TEST - STUDENT COPY - Page two
Have student read from this copy.

No. 3-A

When the man had gone, the boys were surprised to see how many boxes he had left in their little back yard. Right away they began to pile them on top of each other. They made caves and houses. It took so long that lunch time came before they knew they were hungry.

No. 3-B

The man became angry because his dog had never talked before, and, besides, he didn't like its voice. So he took his knife and cut a branch from a palm tree and hit his dog. Just then the palm tree said, "Put down that branch." The man was getting very upset about the way things were going, and he started to throw it away.

No. 4

Three more cowboys tried their best to rope and tie a calf as quickly as Red, but none of them came within ten seconds of his time. Then came the long, thin cowboy. He was the last one to enter the contest.

ORAL READING TEST - STUDENT COPY - Page three
Have student read from this copy.

No. 5

High in the hills they came to a wide ledge where trees grew among the rocks. Grass grew in patches and the ground was covered with bits of wood from trees blown over a long time ago and dried by the sun. Down in the valley it was already beginning to get dark.

No. 6

Businessmen from suburban areas may travel to work in helicopters, land on the roof of an office building, and thus avoid city traffic jams. Families can spend more time at summer homes and mountain cabins through the use of this marvelous craft. People on farms can reach city centers quickly for medical service, shopping, entertainment, or sale of products.

No. 7

The President of the United States was speaking. His audience comprised two thousand foreign born men who had just been admitted to citizenship. They listened intently, their faces aglow with the light of a newborn patriotism, upturned to the calm, intellectual face of the first citizen of the country they now claimed as their own.

ORAL READING TEST
Examiner's Copy and Record Sheet
For Determining Independent and Instructional Reading Levels

Student's Name _____   Date _____

Examiner _____   Class _____

		1st Testing	2nd Testing	3rd Testing
	Date	_____	_____	_____
Total Score: Independent Reading Level		_____	_____	_____
		Grade	Grade	Grade
Instructional Reading Level		_____	_____	_____
		Grade	Grade	Grade

Directions: Student reads aloud from Student copy -- not this copy. If student can't read a word or mispronounces it, just say "Go on", and count it as an error (underline word). Do not tell the student the missed word. Stop the test when Frustration Level is first reached.

			1st Testing	2nd Testing	3rd Testing
No. 1-A (Easy 1st Grade)	Errors	Level			
	0-2	Indep.	☐	☐	☐
	3-4	Instr.	☐	☐	☐
Look at the dog.	5+	Frust.	☐	☐	☐
It is big.	Speed:	Fast	☐	☐	☐
		Avg.	☐	☐	☐
It can run.		Slow	☐	☐	☐
		V.Slow	☐	☐	☐
Run dog, run away.					

			1st Testing	2nd Testing	3rd Testing
No. 1-B (Hard 1st Grade)	Errors	Level			
We saw the sun.	0-2	Indep.	☐	☐	☐
	3-4	Instr.	☐	☐	☐
It made us warm.	5+	Frust.	☐	☐	☐
Now it was time to go home.	Speed:	Fast	☐	☐	☐
		Avg.	☐	☐	☐
		Slow	☐	☐	☐
It was a long way to walk.		V.Slow	☐	☐	☐

ORAL READING TEST -- Continued
Examiner's Copy and Record Sheet
For Determining Independent and Instructional Reading Levels

		1st Testing	2nd Testing	3rd Testing
	Errors	**Level**			

No. 2-A (Easy 2nd Grade)
The door of the house opened
and a man came out. He had
a broom in his hand. He said
to the boy sitting there, "Go
away". The boy got up and
left.

Errors	Level	1st Testing	2nd Testing	3rd Testing
0-2	Indep.	☐	☐	☐
3-4	Instr.	☐	☐	☐
5+	Frust.	☐	☐	☐
Speed:	Fast	☐	☐	☐
	Avg.	☐	☐	☐
	Slow	☐	☐	☐
	V.Slow	☐	☐	☐

No. 2-B (Hard 2nd Grade)
The family ate their breakfast.
Then they gave the pig his
breakfast. It was fun to watch
him eat. He seemed to like it.
He is eating all of it.

Errors	Level	1st Testing	2nd Testing	3rd Testing
0-2	Indep.	☐	☐	☐
3-4	Instr.	☐	☐	☐
5+	Frust.	☐	☐	☐
Speed:	Fast	☐	☐	☐
	Avg.	☐	☐	☐
	Slow	☐	☐	☐
	V.Slow	☐	☐	☐

No. 3-A (Easy 3rd Grade)
When the man had gone, the
boys were surprised to see
how many boxes he had left
in their little back yard.
Right away they began to pile
them on top of each other.
They made caves and houses.
It took so long that lunch time
came before they knew they
were hungry.

Errors	Level	1st Testing	2nd Testing	3rd Testing
0-1	Indep.	☐	☐	☐
2-3	Instr.	☐	☐	☐
4+	Frust.	☐	☐	☐
Speed:	Fast	☐	☐	☐
	Avg.	☐	☐	☐
	Slow	☐	☐	☐
	V.Slow	☐	☐	☐

ORAL READING TEST -- Continued
Examiner's Copy and Record Sheet
For Determining Independent and Instructional Reading Levels

No. 3-B (Hard 3rd Grade)
The man became angry be-
cause his dog had never talked
before, and, besides, he didn't
like its voice. So he took his
knife and cut a branch from a
palm tree and hit his dog. Just
then the palm tree said, "Put
down that branch". The man
was getting very upset about
the way things were going and
he started to throw it away.

	Errors	Level	1st Testing	2nd Testing	3rd Testing
	0-1	Indep.	☐	☐	☐
	2-3	Instr.	☐	☐	☐
	4+	Frust.	☐	☐	☐
Speed:		Fast	☐	☐	☐
		Avg.	☐	☐	☐
		Slow	☐	☐	☐
		V.Slow	☐	☐	☐

No. 4 (4th Grade)
Three more cowboys tried
their best to rope and tie a
calf as quickly as Red, but
none of them came within ten
seconds of his time. Then
came the long, thin cowboy.
He was the last one to enter
the contest.

	Errors	Level	1st Testing	2nd Testing	3rd Testing
	0-1	Indep.	☐	☐	☐
	2	Instr.	☐	☐	☐
	3+	Frust.	☐	☐	☐
Speed:		Fast	☐	☐	☐
		Avg.	☐	☐	☐
		Slow	☐	☐	☐
		V.Slow	☐	☐	☐

No. 5 (5th Grade)
High in the hills they came
to a wide ledge where trees
grew among the rocks. Grass
grew in patches and the
ground was covered with bits
of wood from trees blown over
a long time ago and dried by
the sun. Down in the valley it
was already beginning to get
dark.

	Errors	Level	1st Testing	2nd Testing	3rd Testing
	0-1	Indep.	☐	☐	☐
	2	Instr.	☐	☐	☐
	3+	Frust.	☐	☐	☐
Speed:		Fast	☐	☐	☐
		Avg.	☐	☐	☐
		Slow	☐	☐	☐
		V.Slow	☐	☐	☐

126

ORAL READING TEST -- Continued
Examiner's Copy and Record Sheet
For Determining Independent and Instructional Reading Levels

			1st Testing	2nd Testing	3rd Testing
	Errors	Level			
No. 6 (6th Grade)	0-1	Indep.	☐	☐	☐
Businessmen from suburban	2	Instr.	☐	☐	☐
areas may travel to work in	3+	Frust.	☐	☐	☐
helicopters, land on the roof					
of an office building, and	Speed:	Fast	☐	☐	☐
thus avoid city traffic jams.		Avg.	☐	☐	☐
Families can spend more time		Slow	☐	☐	☐
at summer homes and mountain		V.Slow	☐	☐	☐

cabins through the use of this
marvelous craft. People on
farms can reach city centers
quickly for medical service,
shopping, entertainment, or
sale of products.

			1st Testing	2nd Testing	3rd Testing
	Errors	Level			
No. 7 (7th Grade)	0-1	Indep.	☐	☐	☐
The President of the United	2	Instr.	☐	☐	☐
States was speaking. His	3+	Frust.	☐	☐	☐
audience comprised two					
thousand foreign born men	Speed:	Fast	☐	☐	☐
who had just been admitted to		Avg.	☐	☐	☐
citizenship. They listened		Slow	☐	☐	☐
intently, their faces aglow with		V.Slow	☐	☐	☐

the light of a newborn
patriotism, upturned to the
calm, intellectual face of the
first citizen of the country they
now claimed as their own.

*****

(If the last paragraph is read at the Independent Level,
use a silent reading test to determine advanced skills.)

SILENT READING COMPREHENSION TESTS
Examiner's Directions

How to Administer the Tests. Both tests are located on pages 130 to 139 . If the test is to be administered to a group, make copies of the test on the appropriate level and give each student a copy. (If only one student is taking the test, he may use the test in the manual and write his answers on a separate sheet of paper.) Read the directions below with the students and then tell them to begin:

Read the stories and questions about the stories. You are to read each story carefully and then fill in the space next to the best answer to the question. You may look back at a story if it helps you answer the question. Don't rush, but don't waste time either.

Scoring and Interpretation. These two Reading Comprehension Tests are designed to give you a general idea of a student's comprehension ability in a short period of time. They are shorter than most regular comprehension tests and hence not quite as precise. However, they are a good supplement to a teacher's subjective opinion.

You can tell how your student compares with typical third graders on Test A and with typical seventh graders on Test B. It doesn't make any difference what age or grade your student happens to be.

The Key on the next page tells you the type of comprehension tested (vocabulary, main idea, inference, and so on) for each item, as well as the percentage of students passing the item at grade level three or seven. This gives you some idea of the item difficulty and the kinds of abilities in which your student may be strong or weak.

A total score (total number of items correct) also gives a more general notion of your students' reading comprehension abilities. A total score of 8 correct on Test A would be average for nine-year-olds who would most likely be in mid-third grade. A total score of 7 on Test B would be average for thirteen-year-olds who would most likely be in mid-seventh grade. You can see how your students do in comparison with these guideposts.

Reading comprehension improves with teaching, so teach it for a while using the ideas in this chapter and in the list of Reading Materials. Then retest your students using the Reading Comprehension Tests to see if they have improved.

ANSWER KEY

Test A - intended for nine-year-olds, third grade. A score of 8 correct is average for nine-year-olds, who would most likely be in mid-third grade. It indicates average third grade reading ability.

Item	Answer	Question Type	Percent of Success for Nine-Year-Olds (National Norms)
1	b	Vocabulary	92%
2	d	Reference	63%
3	d	Facts	86%
4	d	Organization	83%
5	e	Main Idea	84%
6	c	Inferences	75%
7	b	Inferences	86%
8	c	Inferences	60%
9	c	Critical Reading	75%
10	a	Critical Reading	75%

Test B - Intended for thirteen-year-olds, seventh grade. A score of 7 correct is average for thirteen-year-olds who would most likely be in mid-seventh grade. It indicates average seventh grade reading ability.

Item	Answer	Question Type	Percent of Success for Thirteen-Year-Olds (National Norms)
1	b	Vocabulary	76%
2	c	Directions	74%
3	a	Reference	68%
4	d	Facts	90%
5	c	Main Idea/Organization	88%
6	b	Inferences	86%
7	e	Inferences	72%
8	e	Inferences	55%
9	b	Critical Reading	56%
10	b	Critical Reading	50%

In each test, the first five questions are literal type questions and the second five are inferential type questions.

SILENT READING COMPREHENSION TESTS

Test A (3rd Level)   Student's Copy

Name _____ Grade _____ Date _____

Read the stories and questions about the stories. You are to read each story carefully and then fill in the space next to the best answer to the question. You may look back at a story if it helps you answer the question. Don't rush, but don't waste time, either.

1. Read the stories and do what they tell you to do.

   ☐ a. **If you have EVER visited the Moon, fill in the box here.**

   ☐ b. **If you have NEVER visited the Moon, fill in the box here.**

2. You want to call Mr. Jones on the telephone. You look in the telephone book for his number. You would find it between which names?

   ☐ a. **Jackson and Jacobs**   ☐ d. **Johnson and Judson**
   ☐ b. **Jacobs and James**   ☐ e. **Judson and Justus**
   ☐ c. **James and Johnson**   ☐ f. **I don't know.**

3. Read the story and complete the sentence that follows it.

   The wind pushed the boat farther and farther out to sea. It started to rain and the fog grew thick. The boy and his father were lost at sea.

   The weather was

   ☐ a. **calm**   ☐ d. **wet**
   ☐ b. **dry**   ☐ e. **I don't know.**
   ☐ c. **sunny**

130

4. Read the story and answer the question which follows it.

> The wind pushed the boat farther and farther out to sea. It started to rain and the fog grew thick. The boy and his father were lost at sea. What happened FIRST in the story?

☐ a. It became foggy
☐ b. It started to rain
☐ c. The boat turned over
☐ d. The boat went out to sea
☐ e. I don't know.

5. Read the passage and answer the question which follows it.

> A sports car differs from an ordinary passenger car in that its size and number of accessories are limited. The sports car also differs from the ordinary passenger car in performance. It can attain higher speeds because it is built smaller and lower. For these reasons it can also turn corners faster and more smoothly than a passenger car. Also a sports car generally gets better gas mileage than an ordinary passenger car.

What does the writer tell you about sports cars?

☐ a. Prices
☐ b. Colors and styles
☐ c. Places to buy them
☐ d. Number of people they hold
☐ e. How sports cars differ from passenger cars
☐ f. I don't know.

6. This is like a game to see if you can tell what the nonsense word in the paragraph stands for. The nonsense word is just a silly word for something that you know very well. Read the paragraph and see if you can tell what the underlined nonsense word stands for.

> Most people have two <u>cags</u>. You use your <u>cags</u> to hold things when you eat or brush your teeth. Some people write with their left <u>cag</u>, and some people write with their right <u>cag</u>.

Cags are probably

☐ a. eyes
☐ b. feet
☐ c. hands
☐ d. pencils
☐ e. I don't know.

7. Read the story and answer the question that follows it.

The wind pushed the boat farther and farther out to sea. It started to rain and the fog grew thick. The boy and his father were lost at sea.

At least how many people were in the boat?

☐ a. One
☐ b. Two
☐ c. Three
☐ d. Four
☐ e. Five
☐ f. I don't know.

8. Read the story and answer the question that follows it.

Christmas was only a few days away. The wind was strong and cold. The sidewalks were covered with snow. The downtown streets were crowded with people. Their faces were hidden by many packages as they went in one store after another. They all tried to move faster as they looked at the clock.

When did the story probably happen?

☐ a. November 28
☐ b. December 1
☐ c. December 21
☐ d. December 25
☐ e. December 28
☐ f. I don't know.

9. Read the story about a fish and answer the question that follows it.

Once there was a fish named Big Eyes, who was tired of swimming. He wanted to get out of the water and walk like other animals do, so one day, without telling anyone, he just jumped out of the water, put on his shoes, and took a long walk around the park.

What do you think the person who wrote this story was trying to do?

- ☐ a. **Tell you what fish are like**
- ☐ b. **Tell you that fish wear shoes**
- ☐ c. **Tell you a funny story about a fish**
- ☐ d. **Tell you that fish don't like to swim**
- ☐ e. **I don't know.**

10. If you listen carefully to what a person says, you can usually tell a lot about him. Sometimes you can tell how he feels.

Read the passage and complete the sentence that follows it.

> **"I'll be glad when this TV show is over. I like stories about spies, not this one about cowboys and Indians. I get to pick the next show."**

The person who said this

- ☐ a. **likes spy stories**
- ☐ b. **doesn't like TV at all**
- ☐ c. **doesn't care what TV show is on**
- ☐ d. **likes stories about cowboys and Indians**
- ☐ e. **I don't know.**

SILENT READING COMPREHENSION TESTS
Test B (7th Level)   Student's Copy

Name _____ Grade _____ Date _____

Below are a number of stories and questions about the stories. You are to read each story carefully and then fill in the space next to the best answer to the question. You may look back at a story if it helps you answer the question. Don't rush, but don't waste time, either.

1. Read the sentence and fill in the box beside the group of words which tells what the sentence means.

   "I certainly won't miss that movie."

   ☐ a. I like that movie
   ☐ b. I'm going to that movie
   ☐ c. I'm not going to that movie
   ☐ d. I hope I'll see that movie, but I don't know if I can
   ☐ e. I didn't see that movie, although it was here all Fall
   ☐ f. I don't know.

2. Read the directions from a can of insecticide spray and answer the question which follows them.

   ### *ABC BUG SPRAY*

   Kills: spiders, roaches, ants, and most other crawling insects. Directions: Spray surfaces over which insects may crawl: doorways, window ledges, cracks, etc. Hold can approximately 10 inches from surface. Do not use near uncovered food or small children. Toxic.

   Which of the following will probably NOT be killed by the spray?

☐ a. Ants
☐ b. Caterpillars
☐ c. Flies
☐ d. Roaches
☐ e. Spiders
☐ f. I don't know.

3. What is the BEST way to find out if there is something about Eskimos in a book?

☐ a. Look in the index
☐ b. Look in the glossary
☐ c. Look at the title page
☐ d. Look through all the pages
☐ e. Skim through the introduction
☐ f. I don't know.

4. Read the passage and answer the question which follows it.

> It should come as no surprise to learn that **9 out of 10** Americans are in debt. In fact, **5 out of 10** are heavily in debt. How heavily is borne out by government statistics that show that income has increased **50%** - while debts have increased **110%!!**
>
> Putting statistics into their proper perspective: paying off the car, the home, the groceries, the doctors and even the children's education is now a way of life for over a hundred million Americans. Very few of us could get by if we had to pay cash when we buy. Keeping up with the Joneses is made easier for us by easy payment plans, easy-to-acquire charge cards, easy-to-borrow bank loans.

According to the article, how many Americans are in debt?

☐ a. **50%**
☐ b. **2 out of 3**
☐ c. **4 out of 5**
☐ d. **9 out of 10**
☐ e. **I don't know.**

5. Read the two stories and answer the question which follows them.

135

STORY 1

A handsome prince was riding his horse in the woods. He saw a dragon chasing a beautiful princess. The prince killed the dragon. The prince and the princess were then married.

STORY 2

Mary was taking a boat ride on a lake. The boat tipped over. Mary was about to drown when a young man jumped in the lake and saved her.

If Story 2 ends like Story 1, what would happen next in Story 2?

☐ a. A prince would kill a dragon
☐ b. The young man would become a prince
☐ c. Mary and the young man would get married
☐ d. The king would give the young man some money
☐ e. I don't know.

6. Read the story and answer the question which follows it.

Sammy got to school ten minutes after the school bell had rung. He was breathing hard and had a black eye. His face was dirty and scratched. One leg of his pants was torn.
Tommy was late to school, too; however, he was only five minutes late. Like Sammy, he was breathing hard, but he was happy and smiling.
Sammy and Tommy had been fighting.

Who probably won?

☐ a. Sammy   ☐ c. Cannot tell from the story
☐ b. Tommy   ☐ d. I don't know.

7. Read the passage and answer the question which follows it.

One spring, Farmer Brown had an unusually good field of wheat. Whenever he saw any birds in this field, he got his gun and shot as many of them as he could. In

the middle of the summer he found that the insects had
multiplied very fast. What Farmer Brown did not
understand was this: A bird is not simply an animal that
eats food the farmer may want for himself. Instead, it is
one of many links in the complex surroundings, or
environment, in which we live.

How much grain a farmer can raise on an acre of
ground depends on many factors. All of these factors can
be divided into two big groups. Such things as the
richness of the soil, the amount of rainfall, the amount of
sunlight, and the temperature belong together in one of
the groups. This group may be called non-living factors.
The second group may be called living factors. The
living factors in any plant's environment are animals and
other plants. Wheat, for example, may be damaged by
wheat rust, a tiny plant that feeds on wheat; or it may be
eaten by plant-eating animals such as birds or
grasshoppers... .

It is easy to see that the relations of plants and
animals to their environment are very complex, and that
any change in the environment is likely to bring about a
whole series of changes.

What important idea about nature does the writer want us to
understand?

☐ a. Farmer Brown was worried about the heavy
        rainfall
☐ b. Nobody needs to have such destructive birds
        around
☐ c. Farmer Brown didn't want the temperature to
        change
☐ d. All insects need not only wheat rust but
        grasshoppers
☐ e. All living things are dependent on other living
        things
☐ f. I don't know.

8. Read the passage and complete the sentence that follows it.

Art says that the polar ice cap is melting at the rate of
3% per year. Bert says that this isn't true because the
polar ice cap is really melting at the rate of 7% per year.

We know for CERTAIN that

- ☐ a. Art is wrong.
- ☐ b. Bert is wrong.
- ☐ c. They are both wrong.
- ☐ d. They both might be right.
- ☐ e. They can't both be right.
- ☐ f. I don't know.

9. Read the passages and answer the question that follows it.

     Johnny told Billy that he could make it rain any time he wanted to by stepping on a spider. Billy said he couldn't. Johnny stepped on a spider. That night it rained. The next day Johnny told Billy, "That proves I can make it rain any time I want to."

Was Johnny right?

- ☐ a. Yes
- ☐ b. No
- ☐ c. Can't tell from the passage
- ☐ d. I don't know.

10.   Read the poem and answer the question that follows it.

My body a rounded stone
With a pattern of smooth seams,
My head a short snake,
Retractive, protective.
My legs come out of their sleeves
Or shrink within,
And so does my chin.
My eyelids are quick clamps.

My back is my roof.
I am always at home.
I travel where my house walks.
It is a smooth stone.
It floats within the lake,
Or rests in the dust.
My flesh lives tenderly
Inside its home.

Which word BEST describes the speaker in the poem?

☐ a. **Confused** ☐ d. **Restless**
☐ b. **Contented** ☐ e. **Unhappy**
☐ c. **Excited** ☐ f. **I don't know.**

This is a sample of a repetitious or "Predictable" story. Try it with beginning readers. Try it with a rap beat.

Busy, Busy Day
by Edward Fry

I got up in the morning and
   I brushed my teeth
   I brushed my teeth
   I brushed my teeth

I brushed my teeth and
   I ate my breakfast
   I ate my breakfast
   I ate my breakfast

I ate my breakfast and
   I went to school
   I went to school
   I went to school

I went to school and
   I met my friends
   I met my friends
   I met my friends

I met my friends and
   I learned to read
   I learned to read
   I learned to read

I learned to read and
   I learned to write
   I learned to write
   I learned to write

I learned to write and
   I wrote my mom
   I wrote my mom
   I wrote my mom

I wrote my mom and
   I wrote my friend
   I wrote my friend
   I wrote my friend

I wrote my friend and
   I wrote my teacher
   I wrote my teacher
   I wrote my teacher

I wrote my teacher and
   I went home
   I went home
   I went home

I went home and
   I played with my friends
   I played with my friends
   I played with my friends

I played with my friends and
   I watched TV
   I watched TV
   I watched TV

I watched TV and
   I ate my dinner
   I ate my dinner
   I ate my dinner

I ate my dinner and
   I read a book
   I read a book
   I read a book

I read a book and
   I brushed my teeth
   I brushed my teeth
   I brushed my teeth

I brushed my teeth and
   I went to bed
   I went to bed
   I went to bed

What did I do today?
I brushed by teeth
I ate my breakfast
I went to school
I met my friends
I learned to read
I learned to write
I wrote my mom
I wrote my friend
I wrote my teacher
I played with my friends
I ate my dinner
I watched TV
I read a book
I brushed my teeth
I went to bed

And I'm tired
Because I've had
A busy, busy day

Teaching Suggestions: Help the student to read this story, perhaps several times. After the student can read the whole story without much help, take words out of context or just point to random words like "school", "teeth", or "met", and see if the student can read them. Practice on a lot of different words. Take some of the practice words and write them on a piece of paper, or a card, or a chalkboard, and see if your student can still read them.